Jean Laplace SJ

PRAYER

ACCORDING TO THE SCRIPTURES

Translated by Mary Louise Powell rc

VERITAS

Published 1991 by
Veritas Publications
7-8 Lower Abbey Street
Dublin 1

First published in English translation by
Religious of the Cenacle
200 Lake Street
Massachusetts 02135
USA

ISBN 1 85390 167 9

Cover design by Banahan McManus, Dublin
Typesetting by Typeform, Dublin
Printed in the Republic of Ireland

Contents

1 Prayer According to the Scriptures 5

2 The Place of Prayer: the Heart 19

3 The Repentant Heart 30

4 The Heart That Cries Out 41

5 The Heart That Remembers 52

6 The Heart That Desires 63

7 The Docile Heart 75

1

PRAYER ACCORDING TO THE SCRIPTURES

The Scriptures: a book of prayer
In religious life today scripture is finding anew the place that belongs to it. Most novices now have their pocket bible alongside their rule book. This does not mean we have no progress to make. There could be an element of passing fad in this renewed interest. Apart from that, you cannot simply hand out bibles and expect everyone to find spiritual nourishment automatically. Perhaps this is possible if most people stay with the Gospels. St Paul is a little more difficult. But what can someone opening the Bible at the first page glean from the stories of the Patriarchs, or even the account of the Exodus? More difficult would be the description of the Sanctuary or the Levitical ceremonial. Any verse of the *Imitation* or a chapter from Father Voillaume would be easier to understand.

Well, then, do we put off the use of the Bible until later, or reserve it as a luxury for prepared and cultured minds? If we were do do either, we should be depriving ourselves of its treasures. The Bible should be a book of spirituality for us and as such should play a role in our formation. In order that it may do this, we must learn how to use it. While we have today many fine introductions and numerous commentaries, it is still hard to find a book which, recognising the progress of exegesis, uses it as a help to savour the text more fully and to draw spiritual profit from it. We have not recovered the inspiration of the first Christian ages which sought God through the Bible itself, and found in its pages the ascetical teaching they needed.

This book is an attempt to do just that. Its subject is prayer, and we are asking the Bible to give us a model and a teaching on this topic. After turning our attention to the heart, which is the place of prayer, we shall describe the paths through which the Scriptures lead the believer in the attainment of the reality: he enters into himself and admits his sinfulness; then he cries out to God to be transformed; thus disposed, he remembers – which is the material for his meditation – and then, under the effect of this remembering, he feels desire aroused in himself. Finally, he attains the end of prayer: docility to God and receptivity to the motion of the Spirit.

Some comments on the advantages of entering the school of scripture in this way are helpful as an introduction before we describe the heart's ascent in its search for God. It would be naive and false to imagine that the Bible renders the traditional ascetical teachings useless – any more than it causes us to ignore the spiritual writers of various ages, or to set the Bible up in opposition to theological effort which finds its principles and rule in Scripture itself. But when we have become steeped in Scripture, we find it easier to recognise the masters of the spiritual life and eliminate the mediocre. The one point that holds our attention, however, is that Scripture gives to all religious training, no matter what 'school' it claims to follow, a balance and rightness sought in vain elsewhere. We shall see this by considering the relish, realism and unity which those who are faithful to its lessons attain in the spiritual life.

Relish and taste for God

We can ascertain the accuracy of these remarks by examining the way Scripture educates us in the area of feelings. It is a fact that in the realm of prayer many distrust any manifestation of feelings. Is it the fault of their early formation or misunderstanding of the words of certain saints? Such persons always believe it dangerous, or at least imperfect, to grant the feelings any place in the spiritual life. They make their dryness or difficulty in praying into a trail borne with courage, when it would be more helpful to look for the causes and remedy the situation. The dryness this attitude sustains in us is only the least of evils. It often leads to psychological deviations of which the person is unaware, which make those around him suffer and damage the effectiveness of the apostolate. We think it is possible to live and turn up our noses at our sensibility, and as a result our psychology is warped and all truly spontaneous gestures are eliminated from our conduct.

According to the Scriptures, a human being cannot downgrade feelings in his relationship with God. Prayer is not an act of mere fidelity. 'I got in my spiritual exercises', a religious often says, as though the satisfaction of having fulfilled an obligation were a consolation for not feeling anything in doing it. True, the scripture does ask us to be exact in the schedule set up for our times of prayer: 'I arose several times, day and night, to sing your praise ...' But this is the fidelity of a lover's rendezvous. No one calculates the time spent to the last second. He satisfies the needs of the heart. 'My soul thirsts for the living God. When shall I see him face to face?' (Ps 42)

Unless these words are said thoughtlessly, out of routine, they presuppose that the one who says them dashes toward God with all the strength of his passions: 'My heart and my flesh cry out for thee, O living God.' The heart speaks to God; that is to say, the most intimate region of my being which makes me myself. But the heart is not satisfied until it communicates its joy to every part of me that can feel it: 'My heart and my flesh ...'. It is as though the feeling for God which catches hold of us is authentic only when transmitted to the least fibre of our being.

For this reason the vocabulary that comes naturally to us in speaking of prayer is that of passion, desire and feeling.

When we meditate on sin or are conscious of the taint that is in us, our features are drawn, we lose sleep, we shed tears and utter sighs. On the other hand, when we feel God's love and protection, a shiver of joy runs through our flesh. We savour the commandments that are our covenant with God, delight in them as in exquisite honey. It is in our flesh that we feel the fear which sometimes comes over us in the face of God's anger or omnipotence. 'My flesh shudders before thee; I fear thy decrees.' The vocabulary through which God expressed his love for Israel is the very same as that used between bridegroom and bride: peace in a love willingly received, or violence in the face of love deceived.

It is not up to a person to arouse these feelings at will. They are the work of grace. But at least in the abandonment or dryness we feel, we can always cry out: 'How long will you hide your face from us, Lord? ... Do not abandon us to the hardness of our hearts ... Deliver me from hidden evil ... Do not let us be delivered into the hands of our enemies ... Give us back the sound of joy and feasting.' This is the weakness of one who finds he can do nothing when God hides himself. If God does not communicate his love and joy to our flesh, we know only too well that we shall look elsewhere for pleasures that bring us fulfilment. 'God of my heart, save me, I wander like a lost sheep. I sigh for you.'

To be bored or in a state of lifeless fidelity before God is not normal. The state will not endure, or if it does, it becomes the pride of the pharisee. The heart that feels arid and longs for refreshing waters – the distracted heart – asks to be recollected once more. A person in this state does not take the blame for it, nor is he satisfied with it because he has done his part through his spiritual efforts. He wants to reap spiritual fruit, the work of grace, but he must ask for it. As a person without an appetite consults the doctor even though he does not feel sick, so the person whose heart is cold begs to have fervour enkindled, and this pleading is itself his prayer.

With the Scriptures as a guide, prayer can no longer be limited to purely intellectual considerations. That is sometimes the danger in meditation books. They make you believe you have spent the time of prayer well if you have had profound thoughts on God, Christ, the Kingdom or the apostolate. 'Until now I thought meditation meant occupying yourself with beautiful thoughts about God,' a young religious once said to me. What is the prayer of the Psalms, if you take them as they really are, but a tireless repetition of the same expressions? You can certainly study the themes they treat, but the list is very quickly made. The one who does not feel things in her heart remains unsatisfied, above all if she imagines that once she has meditated on a subject, she must take another and not return to the preceding theme. The Scriptures give the mind a wide range of material that will keep it in peace during the time of prayer, but they invite it to go beyond the level of human wisdom which reasons and calculates. The Scriptures invite the mind to reach the level of the truth revealed to little ones and the humble, who have nothing but the simplicity of their desire to recommend them.

Anyone who takes time to reflect on these remarks will discover that we have been formed this way for a long time. It's enough to notice the prayers scattered throughout the liturgy to find oneself constantly urged not only to accept the truths of faith but to relish them. Even turning the pages of the missal at random, you can't help coming upon some prayer asking for the divine plenitude: to serve the Lord in peace with a tranquil heart. The whole movement of the liturgy is a call from the Church to go to God not only with the keenness of our intelligence or the acceptance of our will, but with all the powers of feeling or joy within us. There is nothing strange in this. Scripture and liturgy flow from the same stream ... or rather, liturgy, using Scripture only to show us how we can use it ourselves, draws riches from the Bible and becomes our best introduction to it.

To form us for prayer, the Scriptures invite us to gather all our forces. Even as we love the Lord with all our heart, with all our soul, and with all our strength, so we must come to him for this encounter in prayer with our entire being, 'mind, heart, and body', in St Paul's phrase (1 Thess 5:23). Because of the total effort it demands, prayer according to the Scriptures becomes that compact, substantial and delightful reality capable of raising us out of ourselves and leading us to God.

The realism of faith

This stress on feeling may affect us in either of two ways. Some are annoyed while others are delighted. Some cannot escape a certain mistrust, as though this were dangerous ground. Others believe they have been liberated from fears and constraints which in their opinion a narrow training may weigh too heavily on them. For my part, I would like to send both groups away, paired off two by two, saying to the first: in spite of your fears, persevere in search of feeling. And to the second: do not stop at that. The theme of these two opposing counsels is the same: 'Your fear, like your searching, comes from self-complacency. Both need purification. Let yourself be educated further on this point by the Scriptures.'

The case of those who are fearful need not delay us too long. We may add to what was said above: you are afraid of feeling because you don't know where it will lead you. Pray to obtain tears for your faults or joy in Christ. Either is equivalent for you to launching out into the deep. You would like to see where you are going. Sacrifice that desire. Don't be so confident of your own ideas and efforts. Let another tear you away from yourself. If you turn a deaf ear, you unconsciously refuse the only struggle imposed on you

– renunciation of what, according to the circumstances, you believe to be virtue, wisdom or good sense. In reality you are closing the door on the Spirit.

The situation of those who rejoice too quickly at the role given to feelings should hold our attention a bit longer. For of them, too, a struggle is demanded which they do not always recognise easily. To them we must say: this feeling you find so enchanting is ambiguous. According to the advice of St John (1 Jn 4:1) it is not good to trust yourself to it any more than to any spirit at all, whether it be of the religious or apostolic order. There are thousands of examples of possible errors, but two are enough for us here.

Some people say they have the taste for prayer. If you examine this closely, you find that this taste is pure escapism. It is curiously allied with fear of action, annoyance at its daily demands or its 'ordinariness'. This person who speaks of finding God is really finding self. He is escaping a concrete commitment which would make him take stock of his limitations, his egoism, his meanness. He dreams of solitude and balks at the smallest duty. He spends hours in the chapel and is incapable of the smallest service to others. Don't talk to me about his consolations. They are false. The best proof of it is often the lack of taste for any common prayer. Such persons do not like to be with others. It spoils their silence and what they believe to be their communion with God.

For others it is just the opposite. They have, they say, the 'community spirit'. They can pray only when surrounded by others. They feel community. They feel the needs of the world ... they take on themselves its sufferings and interests. Don't talk to them about personal prayer. That's something from another era. Now we pray to the Lord only in a team. They have apostolic consolations which they believe are disinterested because they are directed towards others. They prepare and examine their action in their prayer. Don't be too impressed by either group. Seemingly disinterested, they are absorbed in themselves. Study their reaction when they are contradicted or forgotten. The Kingdom of God grows only in so far as they have something to do with it. If they are ignored, what are things coming to? The future is obstructed and good is compromised.

These portraits are extreme cases, caricatures, but they are not imaginary. We can all see something of ourselves in them. It is painful to admit this because we may discover that the foundations on which we have built our lives are not so solid. So we keep deceiving ourselves. Pseudo-prayer or psuedo-action: the motive is identical ... self-complacency with the illusion of accomplishing good or having generous desires. We must deny ourselves in order to be freed from it, but we usually prefer to erect pious defences against anything that threatens our security.

This is where the Scriptures step in. One of the greatest benefits of the prayer they teach us is to prevent such illusions by establishing us in the realism given by faith. Unless we allow ourselves to go along for years just reciting ready-made phrases without penetrating their meaning, Scripture obliges us to rise above the level at which our feelings seize God and his Kingdom for our own profit. Let's look at this by going back to the two extreme cases described earlier.

First, the unrealistic prayers of people naturally focused on themselves. Scriptural prayer does does not draw us into the interstellar spaces, of which Guardini speaks, where we often claim to encounter God. The Gospel continually places before our eyes the principle by which we are judged: 'Not those who say "Lord, Lord" will enter the kingdom of heaven, but those who do the will of my Father.' And again: 'Little children, let us love in deed and in truth and not merely talk about it' (1 Jn 3:18). To be taken seriously, prayer always presupposes fidelity, or at least the desire to be faithful to something very concrete: the Lord's commandment. To believe oneself good, it is not enough to say we are sincere, that is to say, acting according to what we believe we feel deeply. From this standpoint, who can call themselves sincere? Above and beyond this, we must be filled with rectitude – subject to a rule that dominates us and that we seek outside self. 'It is your will alone to which I cling, Lord.' Furthermore, even though I must pray in my heart, this recollecting of myself is not a withdrawal. I am one among the others. I take my place among God's poor, and though overwhelmed with favours of nature and grace, I recognise that I have no right to consider myself better than any of my brothers. Scriptural prayer is, then, a very realistic and a very 'plebeian' prayer. From this viewpoint, the prayer of certain mystics – while authentic – is more elevated and 'aristocratic'. The prayer of the Psalms always has one foot on the ground. Fastidious people are tempted to expurgate the Psalms in order to bypass the appeals for vengeance or desire for happiness which they see as unworthy of high spirituality. Scripture always brings us back to the need of humble daily actions and to the humble human community.

In the same way we are helped to avoid unrealistic effusiveness in the apostolate and exaggerated 'communal enthusiasm'. The latter applies to those of us who are outgoing, the extroverts. In these also Scripture causes a painful conversion. Their generous sentiments only appear to be divinely inspired. They move on a natural and selfish level. The prayer of the Psalms teaches them to surmount the scandal of the just person who is a failure and to place their trust in God, the only judge. It leads them to discover that the efficiency they dreamed of is not what they thought it was. Above all and most important of all, it forms them to seek God for themselves. Before committing them to action, Scripture invites them to take their own measure and weigh their impurity as though the only true apostolate were founded on the sense of sinfulness. Along with this experience, it places them in the presence of the one and most holy God. Pagans reduce God to human dimensions and are interested in him only in so far as they can use him for earthly religion – something we all risk doing even with the best faith in the world. Scripture however brings us into the presence of this most high God, who wants to raise us to his level and transform us into himself: the God of Abraham and of Jesus Christ, who cannot be seen here below but only in the other world, always farther away, always higher. 'Till now I believed only in human love', a young man told me at the end of a retreat. 'Only that love seemed real to me. I understand now that God's love comes first and human love is real only to him.' This is the kind of discovery that Scripture fosters in the hearts of those whom action turns outward too quickly.

The force of habit must really be great and the defences we raise against all that threatens our ego must be very strong if, after all these years of reciting the Psalms and reading Scripture, we have not gone beyond sentiment. Spiritually, we have remained children, judging things according to the pleasure they give us. This feeling should have helped us to proceed to the faith level, making the invisible real for us; then the feeling would be genuine. We find this in the natural order. A feeling is only genuine when it is directed to another person to whom we give ourselves. If we seek only self-complacency, we vitiate it. The other person is not desired for himself, but for the pleasure he gives us. The same thing applies to our relationship with God or the action we undertake in his service. The temptation to self-complacency always lies in wait for us. Scripture sets about fighting this inclination, which is the forerunner of sin, by having us seek God and his kingdom beyond appearances and present success. Then prayer becomes purifying, inviting us at each moment to go out of ourselves: our works, our failures, our impressions – everything. There is nothing it does not urge us to leave, while at the same time it fills us with relish and zest.

The unifying element of life

Whichever group we identify with – 'wary of feelings or too trustful of them – we shall find there is no 'privileged class' in this matter. Through the effort of faith demanded, we are all faced with the need to experience these things and then to detach ourselves from them and advance beyond them. Sometimes the dangers of too much sentiment or the dryness of faith based on reason will seem better to us than this searing experience which tears us apart. Yet life will be unified and peace assured only in the measure in which we consent to this leaving of self. We experience the paradox of the Christian life: in the poverty of the Cross we possess all things; in nothing – everything. We still have to show how education in prayer through Scripture realises this paradox.

When we propose the annoying question of the unity of prayer and action, we are tempted to seek the solution where it cannot be found. First of all, there is the deceptive unity which gives a comforting feeling of success. Undoubtedly this satisfaction is a valuable encouragement in our efforts. So why belittle it? We feel sorry for the person who never – not even in the first flush of enthusiastic beginnings – feels joy and contentment in the life he is leading. We can predict that, short of a miracle, such a person will not persevere. Still even more to be pitied is one who lives in a naive state of euphoria or swollen pride in work that goes well, or prayer that is without difficulty. The decisiveness of his statements about this makes us suspect that this is the result of the optimism of a good disposition rather than the grace of the Holy Spirit. Others who come up against the problems inherent in action try to solve them on the rational level. They are not necessarily wrong nor does the result have to be bad.

Just as we should be helped by feelings, it is quite legitimate to put logic and clarity into our action. But we must always be revising our solutions; equilibrium can suffer in the measure in which we insist on them. Reason poses the problem, but it still cannot solve it except by renouncing itself to submit to a light and a power which are beyond us. It finds unity in the order of grace.

How is this unity realised in prayer? It is found in the movement which, while it makes us desire the 'feeling' for God and recognises our inability to attain it of ourselves, carries us off in the grace of Christ. According to St Paul, our prayer generally follows the same path as our justification. We are given knowledge and love of the law of God. This revelation and attachment only help us to measure more easily our incapacity to be faithful to him. 'Who will deliver me? .... Thanks be to our Lord Jesus Christ.' I cannot get away from that. It is the movement of my prayer and of all spiritual life. I find the unifying element in the grace of Jesus Christ. 'I have longed for God ... he is my rock ... I love him. I am surrounded by my enemies ... Then I cried out to him and he came down to me ... He has brought me out into the free, open spaces ... In his strength I leap over the wall ...' (Ps 18) ... the wall of all estrangements and weaknesses. First I must know what I am, what I can do and what God proposes to me so that from the depths of the abyss my cry unites me to the Lord. He is the basis of my stability. In success or failure I place myself in God's hands, never despairing, never overly optimistic ... 'He is the only one who has given me many ways of being saved.'

All scriptural prayer finds its unity and its culmination in the movement we have described. It is the first and last movement of all true prayer. Scripture has us follow it from the beginning of conversion, and this continues to be the movement followed by the saint, no matter how advanced he is, unless he wants to fall back into sin. At any stage of life, as long as I stand before God as I truly am, I can believe that this psalm was written for me in this moment of my existence. It is always adaptable to the various stages of spiritual progress. That is why, when I offer it with a humble heart, this prayer produces peace and unity, but does not encourage me to rest in them. Such rest would falsify everything. It would block that movement of perpetual conversion to God which characterises all prayer. It might perhaps bring me a passing consolation, but it would keep me from hearing the 'groaning' of the Spirit drawing me to the Father.

Here we should clarify the way we understand the meaning of peace and unity. Someone who is captivated by the peace experienced and wants to hold onto it or analyse it, is soon disenchanted when all his troubles and anxieties return. This peace is not complete repose. On earth it is often accompanied by the sorrow Christ knew in his Passion, for it is found in the passage from this world to God. Centred in Christ, it knows sorrow but never despair. The paradox of the Beatitudes is realised: laughter in tears, joy in sorrow. St Paul, writing to the Romans, sums up this movement for us: 'Everything written before our time was written for our instruction, that we might derive hope from the lessons of patience and the words of encouragement in the Scriptures.' As long as we willingly accept the conditions of this present life, thanks to the consolation found in the word of God, we shall know peace and hope. Through his Spirit the Lord will fill us with the assurance of eternal life. This hope unifies our mortal lives. We are no longer on the level of sentiment or reason but on that of the workings of God's grace. All our activities, even though tainted, are infused with grace and purified by this infusion.

At the beginning we said that Scripture, in forming us to prayer, gives our lives a balance we cannot find elsewhere. This balance comes to us at Baptism, and we are given a firmer hold on it each time we have recourse to the word of God and the Sacraments. It is a forward impetus because we can preserve it only by our willingness to advance.

This is true for every Christian, but it is indispensable for the apostle today. Our temptation is not to laziness or lack of generosity. It is rather to go under as a result of over-extension or escapism. We need more than ever before a certain quality of prayer – what I have just tried to describe. During a series of days of recollection I gave on prayer, I received a great many confidences from listeners, brought out by the subject treated. Many revolved around difficulties of time, circumstance, peace of mind, etc. 'We have too much work ... we are too scattered ...' and so on. All this is true, but nevertheless, at the end of the series I was left with a certain uneasiness. The real problem is not where we are inclined to situate it, but lies in the absence of this experience of conversion, such as Scripture makes us go through. God must be desired and sought for himself. This will not change life very much – we shall continue to have the same problems and perhaps the same faults – but our outlook will never be the same again. Our hearts will have surrendered. Each time temptation returns to harass us when we are drunk with success, or discouraged by failure, we shall once more go through the same turning of the heart to God. By repeating the same effort over and over again, we finally understand that the solution to our difficulties is found in the interior movement we have described. This is the movement of prayer according to the Scriptures. It becomes our very life.

2

PLACE OF PRAYER: THE HEART

When one person begins to teach another about prayer, she is usually very generous about giving methods and advice. As she tries to solve everyone's difficulties, the teacher provides many exercises and practices. This anxiety to help at least shows the importance attached to prayer. Yet the principle of all prayer established by Christ, to which we must always refer, is forgotten: 'When you pray, go into your room and, closing the door, pray to your Father in secret, and your Father, who sees in secret, will reward you.' Because we fail to start from and return to this, prayer is marked by boredom, routine or falsehood. The first question is not whether we pray best in the chapel, in our room or in the middle of the street, but whether we have ever entered into the heart, the place of prayer. The Father seeks worshippers who no longer adore him here or there, in high places marked in advance, but 'in spirit and in truth ...', that is to say, those who find him in their hearts wherever they may be.

Some find this statement too simple; others, too lofty. The first group say that it is a truth for beginners. The second claims that it doesn't take concrete difficulties into account. These two views only show that both sides have a false idea of prayer, and are seeking in it only self. Sensitivity to this word of Christ is an easy test of the authenticity of what we call prayer. Rather than trying to defend ourselves, let us surrender to this word that it may judge us. Those who understand it truly, find in it the solution to all their difficulties. In its light, we will try to know this secret place where we should withdraw for prayer, the way to find its key, how to remain there once we have entered, and finally, what we find there. First, then, the heart, or the place of prayer; then silence, or the means to enter it; and finally, the Holy Spirit, the gift of God, who teaches us to pray.

'Go into your room....'

What is this room to which we go to find the gift of the Father? The Greek word used here means the storeroom where provisions are kept, the treasury where the money of the state is guarded, a private place where we cannot come and go freely. Many French versions translate your room as *chez toi*. The idea is always the same: the public square is not the place of prayer. You play a role there; you are not yourself. What would this *chez toi* be if not the heart, understood in the biblical sense of the word?

In Holy Scripture the heart does not mean, as it often does for us, the seat of the emotions; it is rather the centre of the personality. To be convinced of this we have only to scan the Psalms or the Gospel and pick out the uses of the word. There we find that thoughts come forth from the heart and the mouth speaks out of its abundance. The heart understands, assimilates, decides and allows us to judge a person in truth. The heart, then, is what makes me myself – me. Above and beyond the intelligence, will and emotions, it is the centre of myself which gives its attention to things, accepts or rejects them. 'Give me your heart', says a proverb (Prov 23:26). The *Jerusalem Bible* translates this as 'Attend to me, keep your eyes fixed on my advice'. In other words, to find me and understand my teachings, give me what is most yourself.

We now understand the two counsels Christ gave on prayer: don't act like the Pharisee; don't act like the pagan. Avoid the ostentation of the one and the babbling of the other. When we speak to God, he is not concerned with the pose we assume before the public. He does not judge us on our reputation – not even our reputation for being religious or not.

Even more – he doesn't stop at the character we play in our own sight, upon which we are tempted to estimate our own inner worth. As St Paul puts it, 'For me it matters little to be judged by you or any other human tribunal. Neither do I judge myself. It is true that my conscience does not reproach me for anything, but I am not justified for that all the same. The Lord is my judge.' I establish myself beyond my role among people, as beyond my psychological consciousness. I strip myself to the essential truth of my being, that 'I' of which I am unaware, or which at least I am incapable of analysing – that by which I am a creature before its creator, a child before its father – at the point where the masks fall.

I must not worry about formulas, not even to keep up appearances. The pagans, who want to 'capture' God for their own advantage, look for magical words. They consider the utility, not the truth of the relationship. 'Don't imitate them', said Christ. Don't be prayer mills. The Father knows very well what you will ask of him before you open your mouth. 'The word is not yet on my tongue, and behold, O God, you know the whole of it.... Wonder of knowledge which is above me, height that I cannot attain' (Ps 139:1-6). At the end of prayer, why are we afraid of not having said or done the right thing? God doesn't need your words at all, still less your dissertations. He does not judge your prayer by the personal impressions that make you judge it as good or bad. What he asks for is your heart: that is, that you accept to be yourself before him. All prayer begins there.

Do not say that there are places or states in which prayer is impossible. Overworked, ill, distracted, even sinful – accept being in the precarious situation that is yours at the moment. Don't wait for ideal conditions, or those you think are ideal. This surrender is yourself. You may not be conscious when you breathe your last. People will no longer see anything. God sees beyond the circumstances. That is enough. You are praying.

In order to enter into prayer, let us begin by understanding something that we must keep telling ourselves over and over: that there is in us an unconquerable citadel where no force, human or diabolical, can enter to drag us out. It is the heart. The devil acts on its surroundings, impresses our imagination, changes our moods. By torture or other methods people tear us apart psychologically. They go so far as to make us say what we do not want to say. But as long as we are conscious, we can be sure that no one can reach that centre of ourself and make us deny what we once said to God and which we renew before him every time it is possible. 'God, you know better than I what I am and what I desire. Nothing will snatch me away from you against my will. You who made me, you know my heart. You alone have given us the key to our heart and it is ours to give to whomever we wish. It cannot be taken from us by force.'

Is it vain to recall this first truth? The religious formalism of the Pharisees and the pagans take turns at lying in wait for us. Either we play a role, or we are afraid of failure. In either case, it is not God we seek. Besides that, we are not ourselves, but we live in the image others have of us, or according to the idea we have conceived of ourselves. To pray, be free: free from others, free from self above all. Free from all poses, all sentimentalism, all overconcern with psychological factors, in the freedom God has given you so that you may be his. From this point of view, prayer is the human act *par excellence*, because it supposes that we know ourselves in true depth. Far from being alienation from self, as many think, it is our true liberation.

'Closing the door....'

We can see now where the difficulty lies in prayer. It is not in lack of time or physical conditions. It lies in this: we rarely descend to the bottom of our heart to remain there. In other words, we are seldom ourselves.

This plain fact is as clear as the turn we give the key in order to shut the door. We pray badly because we are not ourselves, and we are not ourselves because we do not know how to be silent. The condition for all prayer, as for the act of freedom which it demands, is silence. We must rediscover this fundamental truth.

We easily accept this, without realising the depths it reaches. We believe that the effort to be silent consists in halting on the lips the words already formed in the heart – an effort at penance and renunciation which we impose on ourselves once in a while – during a retreat, for instance. This effort is meritorious. Let us hope so, at least. But it remains stiff and forced. It does not quiet the feelings and images constantly bubbling up inside us. We have proof of this every time we come to prayer. The tongue is still, the body motionless, the eyes lowered, but the tranquillity with which we surround ourselves gives free play to the interior 'movies' of restrained thoughts and desires the rest of the time. It is only the appearance of silence. It is not enough to seal the lips, to call oneself silent. Ask the Trappist or the Carmelite. They can tell you about it.

Another struggle is necessary: that which assures silence of the heart. Victory comes only when images, feelings and words no longer trouble us even when we are alone. Is the idea to create a vacuum? A novice in retreat once understood me that way. I don't have to tell you that after three days she couldn't keep it up and her efforts to put aside every thought were driving her mad. Rather than a violent effort to reject everything, this struggle is a prolonged attention to the Lord in a progressive purification of feelings and of every idea. This is education in silence, in the proper sense.

The mystics have spoken of 'nights' – night of the senses, night of the intelligence. Basically, this is what it is all about. If you want to encounter God dwelling in your heart, obviously you can't concentrate on self, even on your most beautiful theological ideas. Complacency kills love and prevents encounter. We have the sad experience of this a thousand times in human relations. We can't truly discover one another because the moment a person is present to us, we develop around her a whole series of feelings and images which subsequently comes between us and prevents us from reaching her. That is why we so rarely say effective words that touch the heart. All true love demands passage through the night, and for even stronger reasons, the love of God who is invisible. To attain it we need images, feelings, ideas, but all this must keep its value as sign and means. When we stop any at self, a dialogue begins – but with ourselves. We no longer hear God's voice. The obstacle is not the distracting image, the captivating feeling, or the absorbing thought. It is our stopping there to enjoy or seek it. We must go beyond, not turn or cross over or pass over, but enter within in order to go beyond. This is the effort in silence necessary for prayer.

This effort demands something more fundamental that we could call human conditioning to prayer, and on the natural level it is connected with the more general problem of attention. With some people we can predict that they will be incapable of undertaking and carrying out a work. They are not in control of themselves; they are the playthings of every passing instinct and imagination. No doubt it is not precise to reduce a person's difficulties in prayer to this psychological instability, but neither should we neglect this aspect. All a human being undertakes in the way of dominating passions and training the attention on the everyday level disposes her to the interior silence needed for prayer. Every worker, no matter what her field, is a silent person – at least in relation to the object to which she applies her efforts. Without silence she bustles around or is bored, and she creates nothing. In the same way, attention to God is impossible without this other self-possession.

We must add that if silence for the sake of prayer finds an ally in this self-control, as long as this self-control is psychologically fragile, it encounters only obstacles in all that draws it to the outside. We wonder how a young person caught up in the whirl of occupations and amusements can form an idea of what true silence is. Guided by fashions and ready-made judgments, burdened with work that is too much for her or that exhilarates, she becomes accustomed to never being herself – and is not aware of it. Even though she is a success socially, she is one of those people – we have all met them and they never cease to amaze us – who are esteemed for the position they fill but who are strangely empty the moment they are alone ... true machines, or robots without souls. Their position in life should not hide the truth. They live without interior unity; their mechanical actions do not express their being because they know nothing of silence.

Conquering the interior powers, refusing distractions ... these are two aspects of natural asceticism which make us accept the silence necessary for being oneself. So much the more should they be found in the asceticism indispensable to prayer. While the heart remains sluggish – now too light, now too heavy – we resemble the broken cisterns of which Jeremiah spoke, letting water escape on all sides. We cannot, in spite of good intentions, live in peaceful, continuous prayer. Rereading the parable of the sower, we must realise that we are not the good ground, rich and silent, capable of receiving the word. Rather we are classed among the superficial in whom the seed does not grow or is quickly choked out. If at least the feeling of going in all directions at once were the first sign of a will to interior recollection! From this emptiness and this abyss we would ceaselessly utter a cry, and that cry would finally bring us unity by driving us towards God. But often we declare that we can do no more, or we even cover up this agitation with apostolic pretexts. In that case, lacking silence, prayer is impossible. Even in our room we are outside of ourselves. 'Lord, help me to gather myself together, to gather myself up in you.'

'Your Father will reward you....'
The petition to 'gather myself up in you' is well put, because the silence of recollection is not emptiness. Thanks to it, I can find God in the depths of my heart – the God who is closer to me than I am to myself. And also – a reflection meaningful for apostles – I meet others there. If this encounter is not illusory, as sensible warmth or intensity of reflection would be, it is because the Holy Spirit himself is the one who brings it about.

Evidently the effort to be silent, if badly understood, can lead to disdain or pride. I am quite aware that at the present time it is not the dangers of silence that are most to be feared. Very few go to excess in this. There is a danger, though, of using silence to create a personal solitude where we escape life and seek self-satisfaction. On the other hand, when we claim that we never have time to pray or can't find favourable conditions for prayer, we are really seeking self, not God. When the demands of silence are met, there is no danger that it will make us concentrate on self or fall into the abyss. In the depths of the heart God is present to welcome us. 'Your Father will reward you...'. He who sees in secret. We are conscious of a presence which is intimate and universal, which no sincere person can escape. We prove the truth of that marvellous Psalm 139 ... 'O Lord, you have probed me and you know me'. The reality of this existence that is mine is God himself: 'Behind me and before, you hem me in and rest your hand upon me.' There is no place, no matter how far away or how hidden it be, where I can escape the One who made me: 'Where can I go from your spirit? From your presence where can I flee?'

This silence in which I settle myself leaves me with only the desire that all may be open before God, to admit of no subterfuge. May I be known completely? I surrender myself to the gaze of the God who is light. 'Probe me, O God, and know my heart; try me and know my thoughts.' This penetration with its dizzying intensity purifies me of all fear and all hypocrisy until I feel it to be creative and loving, and rejoice in it.

When I accept the fact that God lives in me 'in secret', then what Christ said comes to pass: 'Your Father will reward you.' Let us give this phrase its full force. The gift of God, or his response to the appeal of our heart, is the Holy Spirit. To us who do not know how to pray, God sends his Spirit to teach us to call him Father, and to utter 'ineffable groanings' to him. Prayer, as far as it materialises as words, is not our work. If it flows from a pure and virtuous heart, it is the composition of the Spirit in us. 'You are a letter from the Holy Spirit.' It is he alone who teaches us to pray, who bears witness to our spirit that we are sons of God, who teaches us a new language. It is under that action of the Holy Spirit that the movement of prayer described later is worked out. It is he who in turn causes us to enter into ourselves, to weep for our sins, to raise the cry of our heart to God.... He who makes us remember his marvels and kindles desire within us. Thus our prayer becomes one of the deepest expressions of that life of the Trinity which we share. Because we are in Christ, we turn to the Father with the Spirit's cry of love. The exercise of prayer is a distant prefiguration of what we are called to live for all eternity.

So each time we ask for the Spirit we are sure to be heard. That is truly praying in Christ's name: 'What father among you would hand his son a stone when he asked for bread? Or hand him a snake instead of a fish? Or hand him a scorpion if he asked for an egg? If you, then, who are evil, know how to give good things to your children, how much more will the heavenly Father give the Holy Spirit to those

27

who ask him!' This is his special gift which, in Christ, he never ceases to give to hearts disposed to it by silence.

In the depths of this silence we encounter others also. The Spirit who lives in my heart to draw me to the Father is also the Spirit present in all creation, who groans in the hearts of my sisters and brothers or, if they are closed to his action, lends them a new tongue, and acts through their hands. The silence in which we know God is a fraternal silence where there is neither thine nor mine, but where God deep within all of us makes of us one heart and one spirit. Why are there so many who put into strong opposition prayer and action – intimacy with God and encounter with others? Undoubtedly there are practical problems which are difficult to solve. But every human life has its own difficulty. Why do we insist on it so much? If we are so bothered by this point, perhaps it is because we have never looked deeply enough into the reality. Perhaps we have a false conception of both prayer and action, and look for solutions on a level where none exist.

In prayer as in action only silence allows us to find God and not go astray. Only the person who acts risks a failure to feel his emptiness because he is caught up in his work. On the other hand, he who tries to pray without orientation to silence does feel his emptiness. That is why we must insist that an active person pray, for in prayer we feel our poverty. We will find this painful to admit, and will blame the difficult conditions of life. Trials and disappointments in action are necessary to convince us. Yet there is always the fear that the evidence will not be accepted. When it is, liberation of the heart begins. Prayer becomes possible, and action too, at the moment willed by God. The difficulties remain, but the anguish is overcome, for the essential has been recognised.

It all comes back to educating the heart to silence. This is the work of a lifetime, never fully achieved. Those who commit themselves to it risk discovering with amazement that after years of spiritual exercises, they have never prayed in the truth of their hearts. We have stayed on the surface of our being, satisfied with a selfish, sentimental, intellectual form of prayer which gives us only occasional peace. We must push out into the open that uneasiness, ambiguity and discontent existing in the deepest centre of our lives. Let us consent to be ourselves, nothing but ourselves, before God. This is the first stage of a prayer that comes from the heart. It will be described later.

Then we shall discover that this prayer is a simple thing. The mystics – at least the real ones – would tell us we complicate matters unnecessarily. What they do not realise is that this very simplicity is the grace of graces God gives them – something more precious than all other gifts or external miracles. We must ask him to lead us into this simplicity. On that day we shall begin to pray as we should.

3

THE REPENTANT HEART

'If with their whole heart and soul they turn back to you in the land of their enemies ... listen from your heavenly dwelling.' 1 Kings 8:48

The first stage through which the Holy Spirit leads us in order to form us to prayer is that of the heart that repents or returns to God in conversion.* In speaking of stages it is not a question of separate moments. The mind breaks movement down into instants in order to analyse it, but these are only logical moments. In reality we have movement only when it is impossible to isolate its instants. The movement of prayer is like that. Just as in the Liturgy you cannot understand Lent without Paschal time or vice versa, even though one is not the other, so you cannot consider this turning or coming to one's senses without already feeling the atmosphere of love and confidence in which it flowers. If we dwell on self, we are no longer involved in a work of the Spirit, but in a human work. There will be a turning in on self, certainly not an entering into one's self in order to return to God.

Since experience proves it is easy to confuse these two meanings, we should first understand clearly what the Scriptures mean by 'enter into self'. Thanks to our effort to define this we shall have a sure principle to prevent our

---

* The expression *'rentre en lui'* used in the *Jerusalem Bible* is what various English translations render 'repent' ... 'come to their senses' ... 'do penance in their hearts' ... 'come to themselves' ... all ways to convey the idea of entering into one's self to realise one's sinfulness, and returning to God by repentance and conversion.

being taken in by the kind of repentance which causes sadness because it is only exterior. This return or entering into one's self, work of the Holy Spirit, is also a strength from the Spirit which makes us open and pushes us forward.

1. The use of the expression: 'They will come to their senses.' Baruch 2:30

There are many applications of this expression; we choose three where the context is particularly enlightening. An initial text is the great prayer of Solomon after the dedication of the temple (1 Kings 8:30ff). The King describes what God's conduct will be towards his sinful, wilful people. To punish them, God will deliver them to their enemy, but this punishment does not mean that he abandons them. Salvation will be born out of the excess of evil. 'When they sin against you', says Solomon, '(for there is no man who does not sin), and in your anger against them you deliver them to the enemy ... may they repent in the land of their captivity and be converted ... If with their whole heart and soul they turn back to you ... listen from your heavenly dwelling. Forgive your people their sins and all the offences they have committed against you.'

Solomon describes the rule God follows in regard to his chosen people who abandoned him. Moses had already developed this at length in his discourses in Deuteronomy. It is enough to read these, especially the maledictions at the end of the second discourse (28) and the promises of return and conversion in the third (30). The ideal, it says, would be that you walk in the path of fidelity and love. Then you will know joy and blessings. But what person is sinless, as Solomon said. The chosen people – and the people of each one of us – goes on towards its own pleasures and forgets its creator and spouse. God, like a spouse deceived by the one he loves, pursues Israel into the abandonment where its sins have led it. He seeks people in the desert and among the captives. Under the blows of misfortune, the unfaithful one comes to her senses, repents and returns to her creator. This is how God acts towards humanity. He desires only life but if we choose death (apart from God there is only death), God pursues us even there on condition that we enter into ourselves to understand what is happening. 'If they come to their senses, saying we have sinned, then will you pardon them.' That is to say, you will make them return to you.

The second text is like the realisation of the prophecy. It is Baruch 1-3,8, the prayer of the exiles or their confession of sins. This time under the pressure of events the people on the banks of the rivers of Babylon become aware of the absence of God in their predicament, and they confess that they have gone astray. This prayer is so important in what we are considering, and from the point of view which concerns us, that we should comment on it separately. At least let us retain the following thought because it follows the lines of Solomon's prayer: In the land of their exile they will come to their senses and they will know that I am the Lord their God. To sum it up, the punishment we suffer is a sign that You are not abandoning us. It gives rise in us to that first movement of the heart by which, entering into ourselves, we turn to You. It is a pledge of what must follow. You will give us a heart capable of loving You and remaining faithful. In this prayer, the work of the Holy Spirit begins.

The third text is familiar to everyone: the story of the Prodigal Son (Luke 15:11-32). It should hold our attention for a long time because it takes on new value in the light of the first two texts. It is said of the Prodigal as of Israel that he came to his senses under the influence of misery and suffering. In the beginning he was not concerned about fidelity. He only claimed what he considered his rights: 'Give me what is due me.' In his awareness of youthful strength, he thinks only of himself; he demands; he is closed to the world of grace. To be open to it, he must know the loss of all the things in which he put his trust – money, friends, prosperity. When he is deprived of everything, he remembers: I had bread in my father's house. In poverty he knew love. He did not know that what he considered his due was a free gift. Having come to his senses, he knows in one act God and himself. With his goods restored, he no longer claims anything, and nevertheless, he possesses all. In this painful experience the Holy Spirit who sought him out in the depths of evil has revealed grace to him at the same time. It is the beginning of a new life.

2. The beginning of the story of a soul
This story of the Prodigal is at once the story of Israel and of each one of us. Israel, the Prodigal, is all humanity and the individual soul. Each of us, like Israel, is the object of a free election. But at first we are not conscious of it. Seduced by the Satanic temptation, we consider the world our due. 'Take it. This belongs to you', Satan said to Eve in the garden of delights and to Christ in the desert of the temptations. We serve ourselves and for a while live in an illusory happiness. Suffering awakens us and brings us to our senses: this world where we expect to find satisfaction gives only fleeting joy. It is not God. God, our joy, waits for us in this disappointment. Having exhausted evil, humanity turns to the Creator who alone fulfils our desire. In the admission of our misery we see God who has never ceased to wait for us. Feeling the attraction of grace, we surrender to it in the depths of our liberty.

Why this roundabout way to begin to live truly? Couldn't God avoid this and give us from the start the happiness for which he created us? Impossible. Happiness cannot exist in unconsciousness, and if it is imposed it is not true. We ourselves must freely accept the grace which transforms and divinises us. There must be a passage from childhood, in which we enjoy good things without knowing their origin, to adulthood in which we name with love the one who made them. This is the beginning of all spiritual life. No one can avoid it. It is the risk of the freedom which, knowing itself to be created, surrenders to creative love.

Not even our Lady is exempt from this humble beginning. Undoubtedly in her, and conversely in Satan, it lasted the duration of a lightning flash. As soon as she was aware of herself in God, in the awakening of her consciousness, she said 'Yes' to his creative gaze. In this sense she is the model of all creatures, the one in whom we see what we should be through grace: a mirror that opens itself to transparency.

With us things are longer and more complicated. We only reach the beginning of true life after many detours, as the result of sufferings in the land of our exile where we come to our senses and repent. At first we do not know that we are in exile and without God. We feel no hunger for him because the world in which we find ourselves seems to satisfy us so completely. Not that it is bad in itself! God gives us the world to live in ànd to use well, but we make ourselves at home there, settling down to await peace and happiness, when it is a place we pass through as transients. Through the impact of events on us, God has to upset the tower we build to reach the heavens, and bring it down to earth. You do not capture God any more than you can take possession of another person by force. He gives himself to the one who loves him and recognises him for what he is. God gives himself to those who recognise him for what he is – the Unique. As long as he is not thus recognised, we go from one disappointment to another. The series of our falls and sufferings is a kind of constraint which God is permitted to place on our liberty. He does not leave us in peace. Unhappy the rich person for whom everything is successful. God has abandoned that person to prosperity. Happy the one whom God visits in events. As long as it is necessary, he invites us to be beyond self and come to our senses.

What happens, then, in our hearts? We admit our misfortune: in my father's house I had enough to eat. Here I am dying of hunger. Beyond particular failures against the law, we recognise that we have gone astray – an individual or a people stiff-necked, incessantly tempted by idols and the power of nations. we admit that we are children of wrath living in falsehood and error, who do not seek first the justice that comes from God but want to set up our own.

Obviously this clear avowal of sinfulness is not made in a day. It requires long struggles. On the surface the Prodigal left immediately for home. How many days did he hesitate before taking this liberating step! This is not strange. The step assumes that we repudiate the whole direction we have stamped on our lives and hand ourselves over, bound hand and foot, to the One whose existence we have till now tried to ignore, or at least keep at a safe distance. 'I will seek out my father and I will say to him, "I am not worthy to be your son. Treat me as one of your servants."' We understand how hard it is to do this. We also know that God waits patiently as long as necessary. He knows even better than we how much this unique sacrifice costs us, salutary and inevitable though it be. To refuse it is to embed ourselves in pride and despair. If we imagine the Prodigal as unyielding in his misery, refusing to ask for salvation, we will not be very far from hell – if we are not there already.

Perhaps many of us only perform this liberating act at the moment of death – if we do not then refuse it forever. God forces us to weigh the emptiness of our hopes. We no longer possess anything. We see ourselves as nothingness. God permits this painful liberation so that finally the stiff, rebellious creature we are yields to the obvious. In any case, death is a sign of sin. All die because all have sinned, says

St Paul. By death we must recognise that we are outside of God and deliver ourselves up to him, unless once again we rebel and refuse, seeking only self in our nothingness. Then this actually is hell. But for the moment, who can judge the secret of hearts?

Whether it takes place at the final moment or in the course of our lives, this revelation of sin in the depths of our being is the only door that opens on God, or, to follow the parable of the Prodigal, it is the only road that leads to the Father. I must accept the fact that the light of Christ descends into the tomb to visit the dead. No one escapes this view of the abyss from which he is called to the summits of love. Whether I am John, the pure, or Magdalen from whom he drives seven devils, whether I am Peter, the head of the Church, or the thief paying for his crimes on the cross, I must make the same confession. 'If anyone says he is without sin, he is a liar.' Even more, adds John, 'We make him a liar and his word is not in us' (1 John 1:10). Some day or other I must, like Peter, realise the holiness of the One before me and falling to my knees in amazement say, 'Leave me, Lord. I am a sinner.' Or rather I should say like the agonising thief, 'Lord, remember me.' Or simply as the centurion and the Prodigal, "I am not worthy.' Baptism which plunges us into the waters of death is first of all (a condition of the resurrection which follows) the admission of sinfulness and of our powerlessness to clothe ourselves by our own efforts in the robe of the children of God.

Anyone who has not made this admission remains on the margins of the spiritual life. Such a person might be a mature individual with an important role in the world who spiritually, in the best and highest part, remains a child. Such a person will be lucky not to remain that way through stubborn pride. If so, we can only wait in the hope that the impact of misfortune will finally bow that proud head. But along with this example, which is perhaps that of the Elder Son of the Parable, and of the Pharisee, how many so-called

Christian virtues remain weak because they are not founded on this knowledge of self and its admission? Such virtues may leave an impression of purity and fidelity, but these are the purity and fidelity of a child whom contact with reality has never opened to self and to life. I wonder whether this is not the impression that this Elder Son must make. His virtue was pure, but when tested it proved inadequate. He lacked the austere knowledge that he was worth no more than the Prodigal who had wasted his fortune and that his own fidelity was already a grace from God. Far from loving it, he claimed his due – the fatted calf that long service deserved – without recognising that for him also everything was gift.

If this admission of sinfulness is the door to the spiritual life, the test of whether it is real and has cast aside its infancy, we must add that this reaction should continue all through life. Like Baptism, it is only a beginning. As life progresses, we learn from events; as God makes himself known, the sense of our own sinfulness grows. The farther a saint advances, the more conscious he is of being a sinner. The expression of this avowal can change. After the 'Leave me, Lord. I am a sinner,' it can be 'Lord, you know that I love you.' There is no rupture between the two save that of a fall like the denial which only gives us a better measure of the nothingness from which God is continually saving us.

3. The work of the Holy Spirit
In the course of a retreat a Catholic Action militant once said to the preacher who invited him to meditate on sin, 'You are dampening our enthusiasm for action with such subjects. Have us make more optimistic meditations.' How many others say this each time they touch the matter of sin! It makes them feel only sadness. Yet you cannot live in love if you do not linger over these austere truths.

The danger is very real. How many find in meditation on sin simply an occasion for self-deprecation and from this, discouragement. It is there precisely that they are not following Scripture. If they were schooled by it, Scripture would have taught them to distinguish this entering into one's heart from its counterfeits.

If we were referring to a turning in on self when we say, enter into one's heart, then the best psychologist would be surest of accomplishing this first stage in all prayer. But psychological introspection has no place here. It leads to pride or despair. Revealing the secret motives of our aversions, it still encloses us in our solitude. The self-knowledge the Holy Spirit breathes into us in prayer is less detailed. Perhaps it is an analysis that cannot be put into words. It is that massive, almost intuitive global view of self that we take when we are in God's presence. Along with it there is a consciousness of the holiness and purity of God which draws us, and, entering into ourselves again, we find him in us – 'more ourselves than we are ourselves.' As cruel as it may be – 'I have sinned against heaven and against thee'– it never leaves us alone. God is present in it, forming it within us and giving us the strength to bear its severity. It makes us realise our corruption as a whole and the need we have of Jesus Christ. In the same act I know my sin and my Saviour. That is why the feeling which accompanies it – what we call compunction – unites the most opposite attitudes: sadness, surely, but not that of the world which brings death – rather that which is according to God and produces salutary repentance (2 Co 7:10). The best description we could have of this is the feelings of David after his sin, either in 2 Samuel or in the transposition the Psalmist gives of this sorrow (Ps 51), 'Have pity on me, Lord, in your goodness.' Strange accents of joy and confidence are mingled overwhelmingly. The bones crushed by sin dance for joy under the breath of the Spirit who recreates them.

Thus, before rejecting this prolonged attention to our sinfulness as pernicious, be careful to distinguish between entering into one's self and turning in on self. Without the distinction, the militant risks being deprived of the greatest of benefits, and of exercising an action that is Catholic in name only. This acknowledgement of sinfulness as we have described it is the indispensable foundation of all spiritual as well as apostolic life. Without it both run the risk of developing an illusion.

The mark of authentic piety is first of all this same humility. Just as the self-denigrating person who risks being interested in self alone, believing he is humble, so also the one who is afraid to dwell on this admission risks loving only self, even if the pretext is love and confidence. God's gaze resting on me pierces my darkness and the more penetrating it is, the more it confuses me. True purity does not avoid passage through these painful regions. So long as it is mere ignorance, purity is not the work of the Holy Spirit but the natural delicacy of the sheltered child.

The apostle who has not gone through this experience or does not found zeal on it, is not to be admired too much. The one without the other is, most of the time, only the expression of an overwhelming ego. This is easily proved in time of contradiction and trial. Only the person who knows from the experience of his own weakness that it is God who does all things through the power of his word, resists the intoxication of success or the discouragement of failure. Only those of us who have faced up to our sinfulness can know for ourselves and teach others from what evil God saves us. Lacking this we will do only a work of human goodness, not the work of salvation. Finally, only those who in this entering into the heart learn not to believe themselves better than all the prodigal sons, can love others with something different from the protecting kind of love which makes the other feel all the distance separating that person from us. To love each other as brothers in Christ, we must first know each other as equally saved in him.

We can pick up again the words of the Catholic Action militant and measure – thanks to these reflections – the distance which separates them from the love of God and the love of humanity. There is no question of a person's generosity, but it is not enlightened. It remains on the natural level, in a failure to realise that this admission of sinfulness, like all prayer and every apostolic work, is born of the action of the Holy Spirit. We should not fear it as a handicap to love or action. Produced in our hearts by the Spirit, it bears his seal: peace, confidence, joy. There is no danger of complacency in it as there can often be with people for whom a certain dramatic way of acknowledging their sins is just one more way of concentrating on self. We know ourselves as sinners only in the grace of God, in the abyss of the mercy which saves us from sin. The Spirit who makes us enter into ourselves also draws us out to surrender us to God. To stop at the first stage would be to block the movement of the Spirit.

From this analysis we see the nature of this education in prayer. It is a movement which carries us beyond ourselves. It is not surprising if in this avowal of sin we find the seed of joy and love. God is present and known in the knowledge of self which he inspires in us. The strength of this contrition is the sign that it is not the work of unhealthy sensibility. The Spirit working in our hearts cleanses the stains, waters what is dry, heals what is wounded. To take up the great image from Ezekiel and the Psalms, it is he who breathes on the dust to which we are reduced by sin to create anew what no longer exists, and renew the face of the earth.

4

THE HEART THAT CRIES OUT

As the Prodigal Son returns to his father's house, it is easy to picture him turning over in his heart the verses of Psalm 130: 'Out of the depths I cry to you. Lord, hear my call.' Reading these verses over in their entirety shows how exactly they fit his situation. The Holy Spirit, who makes us enter into ourselves to admit our sinfulness, draws us out of self to cry out our need for grace. Each cry is a step towards the Father, who wants to teach us the marvels of his love.

With the avowal of our sinfulness, this cry which the Scriptures have us utter to God to beg for his grace is the indispensable preliminary for all encounter with God in prayer. Many omit it, and so their prayer is only a tissue of reflections without power to enkindle and transform the heart. The master-touch of grace is necessary, and they feel no need of it. Such prayer is not inspired by the Spirit.

The school of Scripture teaches us that time spent harassing the Lord with these cries is not lost. We must pass from the natural level to the level of grace. By means of a few examples of typical prayers, we can see how this passage takes place. We dispose our hearts for it so that God may accomplish it and guide us. From the analysis flow several conclusions on the character which development into this second state – the heart that cries out – gives our asceticism, and our spiritual effort.

The need for grace
To affirm the need for grace in teaching catechism is one thing, but to experience it is quite another. This is the experience which Scripture presupposes in the texts to be

quoted; the first, Isaiah 63:7-64:11 – the feeling of hardness of heart.

This long psalm is a recollection and an appeal. It lists the kindnesses of God in the past and tells how he has been Saviour to his people. But today it is all over: 'See, see, we are all your people; your holy cities are a wilderness, Zion a wilderness, Jerusalem a desolation.' Why this change? They have revolted. They have saddened his Holy Spirit. Then – these are the words that should make us pause: 'Why have you let us stray from your ways and harden our hearts against fearing you? Return, for the sake of your servants...' And further on: 'We were all like men unclean, all that integrity of ours like filthy clothing... For you hid your face from us and gave us up to the power of our sins.'

The absence of God I experience because of sin makes my heart like stone. When God turns his face away from me – that transforming face in whose image I am made – he sends me back into my natural opacity. Now, coming to my senses under the pressure of suffering and exile, I would like to escape from this condition, and I feel incapable of doing so. In spite of my shame and my good desires, I do not do the good I want to do, and I keep on doing the evil I do not desire. I feel as though a weight drags me along – that power of our evil deeds which St Paul describes in Romans. There is a fatal unfolding of them that I cannot halt. I am delivered to sin as to a power stronger than myself.

There is just one means of breaking this deadly stream: free supplication. Do not abandon me to myself, O my God. Melt the hardness of my heart. Do not trust me out of your sight. To know that we are hardened is to feel already the radiance of God's face shining upon us. 'For who can free himself from his poor ways and his poor limits if you do not lift him up to yourself in the purity of love, my God?' (St John of the Cross).

In the Missal, the prayer for tears puts it so well: 'You make tears of compunction spring out of the hardness of my heart.' I do not take credit for a feeling I do not have, or if I have it, I recognise its author. Of myself I am naturally hard. If the need to break the rock that is myself springs up within me, that very need is the Spirit's work. The feeling of domination that presses on me becomes my salvation on the day when it impels me to beg for help. The sin in which I am so enclosed that I feel its weight upon me makes me cry out to God to re-fashion me. 'Do not incline my heart to evil works' (Psalm 141:4).

The face of the Lord – Baruch

Again it is the inclinations of the heart – the 'slopes' – that the prayer of Baruch evokes: 'Each following the dictates of his evil heart, we have taken to serving alien gods and doing what is displeasing to the Lord our God' (Baruch 1:22). Two forces or two loves woo my heart: these are its 'slopes'. On one side what is natural for me drags me toward self and to the bottom. I can picture myself with all human generations descending into hell, far from God. St Teresa of Avila saw her place there. Each of us can do as much. It is not the work of a sick imagination. If we are left to ourselves, what can we do but fall under our own weight? On the other side, the force of the Holy Spirit which God breathes into me when he looks upon me, draws me to him.

What should I do to be carried away by the second force? (There is no third choice.) I do not have the power to lay hold of it for myself. He who says, 'I shall be like God,' is like Satan, who wanted to 'go it alone'. I can only beg the Lord to look at me. Invocation of the face of the Lord is frequent in Scripture. If it turns away, I return to my nothingness. If it looks on me, hope is reborn. 'We will be like him because we will see him as he is,' says St John. Therefore, if I feel that I am far from God, with no attraction to good, there is one reproach I can always make to myself, the same self-reproach of the Exiles: 'we have not entreated

43

the face of the Lord.' By my own efforts I cannot escape my evil and acquire the virtue that makes me pleasing to God. But I can always turn to the Lord, asking him, in the translation of the Crampon Bible, 'to turn each one of us away from the thoughts of his evil heart' (Baruch 2:8).... on condition that I at once recognise that this glance I cast up to the Lord is only the response to what he asks of me.

Psalms and Prophets: 'Create in me a pure heart'

What I expect from God is more than a simple purification; it is a complete re-fashioning. 'Create in me a pure heart, O Lord,' Psalm 51 begs. All Scripture echoes this plea. Nothing in our 'complicated heart' (Jeremiah 17:9) escapes the Lord's gaze. As he sounds the abysses and can dry up the heart of the seas, so he can turn us inside out to make a new creature of him. 'I will give you a new heart...' (Ezekiel 36:26,27). This text is the strongest expression of that divine transformation of heart which the inspired men of the Old and New Testaments described in such enviable passages. Jeremiah, Baruch and the Psalms take up the same words. With St Paul we beg that we may not be delivered to the desires of our hearts (Romans 1:24) but that the Holy Spirit may imprint on the tablets of our hearts that likeness to his Son which is part of the Father's plan for us. We are, he says, 'A letter from Christ, drawn up by us and written not in ink but with the Spirit of the Living God, not on stone tablets, but on the tablets of your living hearts.'

If there is, then, some fidelity in virtue, it is fitting to know who the author is. God is himself our fidelity, and it is he who works within us both the desire and its fulfilment. 'We are God's work of art created in Christ Jesus to live the good life as from the beginning he meant us to live it.' God has promulgated his law. Yet while it remains something external, written on stone tablets, it is our condemnation. It shows up our evilness, but leaves us to our powerlessness. It calls forth the admission of our sins, but does not correct us. God must transform my heart if it is to follow his law and delight in his commandments: 'Reflect on the injunctions of the Lord ... He will strengthen your mind' (Ecclesiasticus 6:37). The Psalms and Wisdom describe this metamorphosis in detail. If we re-read the great psalm of the Law, 119, we see that far from being an act of confidence in virtue based on pharisaical pride, it is – especially in verses 33 to 80 – an insistent crying out for the grace that makes for fidelity. 'Around me the enemy jeers .... Let me take pleasure in your commandments .... Give me understanding that I may keep your law and observe it wholeheartedly ... Incline my heart to your commandments ... Turn my eyes from vain things ... Make me live in your justice ... Have pity on me according to your word ... May my heart be without stain so that I may not be overcome.'

Prayer cuts short all self-sufficiency. Fidelity to the commandments, appeasement of the heart's passions, ardour in serving God can only be the work of the Holy Spirit. Most to be feared is the pride of heart which attributes merit to itself instead of recognising the One who ceaselessly renews us in the image of our Creator. 'What man can say, "I have cleansed my heart, I am purified of my sin"?' (Proverbs 20:9). To the very end saint and sinner alike beg: 'Create in me a pure heart.'

The prayer of Solomon: the request for wisdom – Wisdom 9

No better expression of this faith in creative grace in our hearts can be found than the prayer of Solomon asking for Wisdom. It is so rich that, like the prayer of the Exiles, it demands a separate commentary. We can at least indicate the essence of the attitude it presupposes.

To seek wisdom is to seek perfection, to seek God himself, for she is 'a breath of the power of God, pure emanation of the glory of the Almighty.' How then shall we take her to ourselves and live in friendship with her?

In this quest of the precious pearl, natural virtues are no help. Solomon possesses them and with them all that we can desire on earth: a well-formed body, natural happiness, a good mind, all the qualities the pagan cultivated to become a complete person. But I understood, Solomon said (and to understand it was a grace), that possession of this human equilibrium did not give me the right to claim wisdom. That is obtained only as a free gift from the One who possesses it. You do not merit it by your own efforts; go ask for it as a gift. To obtain it, I did not cross seas or scale mountains like the traders or heroes of whom Baruch speaks. I turned to the Lord and spoke from the bottom of my heart.

We can summarise our effort. 'Man's heart seeks his way, but it is Yahweh who strengthens his steps', reads the Vulgate translation of lines from Wisdom. In the presence of grace, we are not reduced to a soft *laisser faire*, which is actually lack of confidence in the nature God has given us to help us move toward him, and in the grace he offers us to transform it. But we cannot produce in ourselves the virtue whose ideal and desire God inspires in us. Only God can give strength and joy. It remains for us ceaselessly to dispose our hearts. You have the impression that God is not with you? Say to the Lord: Look upon me. Harden not my heart. Create in me a pure heart. Then, when he wills, God will give you his wisdom – undoubtedly not in the way you expect. Perhaps he has already gifted you with it, but you cannot yet recognise it.

After looking at these texts and drawing conclusions, it would be fruitful to read again, in St John, Christ's counsel on prayer, especially the discourse after the Last Supper. Two expressions will hold our attention: 'Until now you have not asked anything of me,' and again, 'Everything you ask of the Father in my name, he will give it to you.' Not that the Apostles had never really asked anything of the Lord: the sons of Zebedee had even asked for the first places in the Kingdom, but they had not asked in the spirit of one who requests wisdom. They became attached to false wisdoms: 'When will you establish the Kingdom?' 'You know not what you ask', is the reply. They were seeking other goods, not the ones he brought. They did not know their deep need of his grace.

We begin to pray in the name of Christ when we have contemplated him in the Passion becoming our justice, and realise how true it is that without him we can do nothing. We still have not prayed in his name, and we still have not asked anything of him – so much so that in the depths of our hearts we have not felt how vain our virtue really is and how truly the fruits we bear are his in us.

Grace and asceticism

This re-creation of the heart, as the Scripture describes it, to make it the seat of wisdom, is a precious aid to a better understanding of the counsels of traditional asceticism. There is no question of rejecting them as though we had to invent a new spirituality for our time. If they have produced in us the opposite of what we expected – made us rigid instead of flexible – it is often because we have failed to situate them properly. The great benefit of the Scripture is to infuse into us a very sure instinct which, without rejecting anything, helps us put each element in its proper place. Here are some examples.

1. Sufficient generosity

There are Christians who remain insensitive to meditation on sin and the request for spiritual goods. It is not that their lives lack generosity. On the contrary, they are austere and devoted. It is as though there were a dimension lacking in their lives.

I never felt this quite so keenly as during a retreat for older pupils in an excellent Christian school. They came from a good environment. Despite certain difficulty in submitting to the time for prayer that I was asking, the retreat was going well. On the first day I had spoken of Creation and our place in the universe and before God. Everything changed the second day when I placed them in the presence of sin. I felt like a jet taking off while the passengers remained on the field. They were not with me. The reason was very soon obvious, and certain confidences in private talks proved I was right. I had entered into the exclusive domain of grace where we all must feel within the need to be saved, and give ourselves up to Christ. These young people had never counted on anyone but themselves. They had never had any need to do otherwise. Their virtues, which did not 'shake them up' at all, save for the peccadilloes of which they accused themselves in confession, remained natural.

This can be frequent in religious persons, especially those for whom good education assures a balance of natural virtues, and spares from the hardest shocks of life. The cry has never sprung from their hearts. They have known only those tranquil prayers which kept them in a quiet atmosphere without disturbing them. They remain insensible to the cry of the Psalms. Although they may have made pilgrimages, always fulfilled spiritual obligations, Christ can say to them: 'You never asked anything of me. You did not need me as a saviour. You never called to me for help. Like Simon the Pharisee, you did not believe that you needed to have many things pardoned you. And so you were scarcely open at all to love.'

2. Discouraged generosity

This case is probably more common, since tranquil and undisturbed youth is becoming rare. It is the case of those young people for whom the reality of their own being and the world is a daily contradiction of the ideal they have dreamed. They feel their powerlessness or the harshness of life. But their first failures offer no occasion to call on someone else to help them. They are closed up in themselves and incapable of breaking out. Since they want to depend on their own efforts for everything, their generosity only supplies occasions for discouragement. At the end, they give it all up and fall into the evil they tried to avoid from the start.

What is missing here? Exactly what the first group of people lack. They are getting in their own way. they do not know what it is to hand oneself over to Jesus Christ to be saved by him. Every director of conscience has had this painful experience. Many young people cannot get rid of bad habits because they see them only as a blemish which destroys the idea they have of themselves, rather than the obstacle which prevents them from giving themselves and loving. The admission of sinfulness is for them only an occasion for becoming dejected.

To get them out of this state, you must help them to mature. In spite of the anguish that agitates them or the questions they ask themselves, they have remained adolescents in the sense that they live turned in on themselves. They must become capable of gift. Only then will the obstacle become a means for them. They, too, perhaps more quickly than the other group, will feel their need of being pardoned much. On that day they will begin to pray in the name of Christ whom they know as Saviour.

3. The eagerness to do well

Many get off to a bad start because they have not felt the need for grace deeply enough. Others who seem to start off well see their enthusiasm fade because along the way they take back the gift of self and grow to count more on themselves than on Christ. They become impatient and discouraged. It is not an exaggeration to say that this is the greatest common obstacle to perfection. Great courage is needed, but it has to be applied at the right spot. Many spoil the work by eagerness to do it themselves. They are like St Peter wanting to follow Christ on the condition of giving him advice: 'This can't happen to you, Lord!' Or again, feeling the monotony of it all after the exciting discoveries of their first stages, they believe they are not advancing further and become uneasy, as though the obsession with doing badly or doing too little were the sign that all is well with them. Actually it indicates that we are still very much attached to ourselves and that God is not yet someone to whom we have surrendered.

So God leaves us to our unconscious self-sufficiency. That is his way of curing us of it. Perhaps when we realise we have got things all wrong, or when a fall like St Peter's reduces us to helplessness, our heart, freed by the admission, will open to grace. At any rate, as the days pass without bringing success, we must not let the certainty we had in the beginning weaken. No matter what happens, let us pray as Christ did in the Agony – as the Apostles did not. We will profit much by this effort: only this opens us to God. Many jeopardise it all by indiscreet haste.

4. Peaceful effort
All this finally brings us to a definition of the only kind of effort by which we find God: the effort we make in grace or – to put it better, playing on the words – with grace. There is no mistake here. The sign that our asceticism is Christian is that it sacrifices nothing of the ideal of its beginnings, while at same time it remains peaceful in the effort to attain it. While those whose virtue counts on itself become hard and sceptical with age, Christian asceticism allows one who matures in grace to retain the freshness of youth even while losing its illusion. It is a moving experience to remember persons whom we have seen grow old before us, but in whom age did not dim the gaze nor dull the bright edge of their peace. Thanks to them we can guess something about our Father in heaven. It was neither candour nor ignorance

that kept them like this. They had no illusions about humankind. But their faith in the grace that made heaven's first citizen out of a penitent thief was stronger than any other evidence. May their example at least teach us something. We shall not stop asking God for these very holy gifts, or a little of the love which, as St John of the Cross says, is worth more to the Church than all works put together. Hopefully, we will also realise that to secure this, straining the nerves and splitting the head are useless. We must simply never stop asking, never give up trying, and thanks to prayer, our efforts will be sweet and blessed by God.

To conclude, a word that summarises what preceded and announces what follows: in forming us to prayer, Scripture renders the soul malleable to the action of the Holy Spirit. Only the Spirit who knows God's secrets reveals them to us. His paths are at once sweet and austere. They are those of grace, which is daily created in us and prevents us from resting on our laurels. Our effort must be unceasing. It must be an effort which has its beginning and end in Jesus Christ.

5

THE HEART THAT REMEMBERS

Silence of heart, admission of sin, plea for grace: we must never enter into prayer without these preliminary stages taught by Scripture. Otherwise we will be like the novice who told me that after five minutes of meditation, he didn't know what else to do.

'I've exhausted the material.'

'But how do you go about it?'

'I read over the notes taken at the instruction and reflect on them a bit.'

'Sitting or kneeling?'

'Sitting or kneeling?' He obviously found it a bizarre question. 'Sitting', he told me.

'You don't begin by placing yourself before God and asking his grace?'

'No.' He had not begun to pray but to think. That is why the result was so pitiful. He understood it better later on.

For those who wish to learn to pray, it is a question of discovering in Scripture what every spiritual master has always taught: you do not enter into prayer as though you were right at home. Before the burning bush Moses took off his shoes and fell prostrate. We must do the same in prayer. It is a divine activity – that of the Spirit in us. We do not approach it as though the result depended solely on us. We dispose ourselves for it, as we do for grace, by respectful attention.

A second remark helpful in what follows is that the three stages described earlier do not constitute an escape from life, even though they demand retreat from our occupations and independence of heart. On the contrary, if some people feel ill at ease in them or think lingering over them useless, it is because such persons lack the maturity this experience brings. The prayer of Scripture, especially the Psalms, could be an occasion for artistic pleasure or something to which we are attached out of snobbery. To avoid this and to savour the prayers cited in the following examples, we must know what we are before God, and have felt this in ourselves – even at the cost of painful failures and humiliating falls. We need to have passed through the trial and to have accepted what it teaches.

So these preludes are not recipes for novices or arbitrary complications which a true spirit of childlikeness can bypass. No matter how these preliminaries are expressed, they translate the fundamental laws of our encounter with God, and they are valid at all ages of life. If we neglect them, we shall really be addressing ourselves not to him but to an idea built up by our own desires.

This stage is only a point of departure, however. Aside from a special grace which suspends us in silence or holds us in the avowal of sin, we risk finding a void when we have stilled ourselves. At the beginning of a retreat a retreatant who had heard me talk on silence of heart was forcing himself to think of nothing. Needless to say he was going round in circles. After gathering us up in recollection and putting us in our rightful place before God, the Scriptures offer an object for our consideration. Meditation begins here.

This object is offered first to the heart that remembers. Memory is necessary to pray in the school of Scripture. It is one of the believer's key faculties. The unbeliever is a broken cask which does not remember but lets memories run out. The wise person stores in her heart the words heard in order to understand them and apply them to herself.

What do we remember?
Everyone who has taught others to pray has spoken of the need to prepare for it. Scripture asks the same of us,

soliciting an effort of our attention and memory. 'Listen and write this in your heart and may it penetrate even to the tranquil foundations of thought.' (Claudel)

Naturally, I do not apply my memory to just any object. We could learn much from picking out in the Bible the various things proposed for our meditation: 'They did not remember the multitude of his mercies' ... 'I remember that there is not justice save in you' ... 'I have remembered your name' ... 'I have not forgotten Your commandments ...'. Your marvels, your name, your unique holiness, your law: each of us can continue the list according to personal taste and reading.

What is worth noting is that this proposed meditation bears directly on facts and events. It does not consist in arousing sentiments or losing ourselves in learned reflections. Many meditation books open false paths to us on that score. They put us into a ready-made world where we are engrossed in our own ideas or those of other people. This is the origin of the artificial sugary language such books often inspire in their users. More nobly, perhaps, others take articles from the *Summa* for meditation or use material from theology courses. The result is the same. They settle down among their own ideas and images. True prayer supposes that you go out for yourself and humbly submit to something given. The believer, like an actor who learns his role, first puts words in his own mouth. He repeats them to himself hoping that little by little understanding will be given to him.

Time plays an indispensable part in this assimilation by the memory. The Liturgy, inspired by Scripture, knows this well, for it continually repeats the same texts to us. This is because it knows the rhythm necessary for the development of faith. A word becomes ours only at the point where we believe we recreate it in ourselves, and only if we take time to listen to it and repeat it. What difference does it make if I'm assailed by distractions or little disposed to be deeply moved? I take the Book and gently, without wearying, repeat the same words or review the same events. I ask God to make me understand them, to imprint them in my heart. There is the beginning of real prayer even if the hour has passed and I have to admit that once again I slept through it or felt nothing. Actually, the Word has penetrated my heart. It will blaze its path there.

There are thousands of possible examples of this way of proceeding. The style itself seems monotonous to one who goes through the Bible without becoming involved in its dynamism. Each time a prophet, an apostle or a believer wants to obtain some favour from God or simply to be in his presence, he sees again in his thoughts the marvels accomplished by the Lord, as if in his present difficulties – surrounded by enemies as Judith was, threatened with death like Esther, persecuted like the Maccabees – the person of faith can take courage only by going back beyond the Flood even to the creation of the world. This is the same type of consideration that St Peter proposed to the Christians who were shaken by the mockery of their enemies, surprised that the coming of Christ had not changed history at all (2 Peter 3:3-7). To make our faith in the world come secure in the present moment, we need to remember all the past.

The central theme of meditation continually suggested to the Jewish heart is obviously that of the Exodus: the memory of the marvels God accomplished for his people, the sign of those he will still work. To the end of his life, to the end of time, the believer does not tire of singing the Great Hallel which is typical of prayer inspired by these events: 'Give thanks to the Lord, for he is good; his love is everlasting. His wisdom made the heavens; his love is everlasting. He struck down the first-born of Egypt ... and brought Israel out. His love is everlasting.'

The Christian receives the same meditation theme: the creation and redemption as signs of God's love and the good things he prepared for those he loves. But in the evoking of the figure the Christian sees the reality. In the Exodus we contemplate the mystery of deliverance through Christ: Passion, Resurrection, Ascension, Pentecost, the life of the Church as it waits for his second coming. The Pasch is no longer the lamb eaten as a meal for travellers, the blood of which protected the sons of Israel. In the one who gave his life for us and who reigns forever, the Pasch is a memorial of the past, possession of the reality and announcement of the future. And so the Christian's prayer spontaneously takes the form of a wondering enumeration. In the same way popular devotion has created the Way of the Cross and the Rosary. We might think their form a bit rigid, but the principle is good. Each person is free, anyway, to do as the master glassmaker of the twelfth-century west door in the Cathedral of Chartres. He proposes a real Via Crucis to us, leading our gaze from the Transfiguration to the manifestation at Emmaus by way of the Last Supper and the Cross. By walking tranquilly through a cathedral we grasp more easily the kind of prayer that flows out of Scripture. It is carved there in stone, from Genesis to the Apocalypse. From this point of view we can understand the advice of the saints to meditate habitually on the Passion. In it they felt themselves at the heart of God's wonders. They came back to it again and again after the example of the Evangelists, who devote more pages to these twenty-four hours than to the infancy or the public life. Again, in reading the Psalms they referred to the death and Resurrection of Christ. When the saints consecrated the Eucharist they always reached the same marvels through the signs.

The Liturgy appears to be here the best way of initiation into Scripture and into prayer. But how will its action be exercised if we do not take time, according to the grace God gives us, to remember these things often and to ponder them in our hearts?

How to remember

The meditation Scripture suggests is not intellectual, nor is it mere passive reading carried out in the hope of receiving enlightenment. It requires attention to events, not ideas, and demands that these events become present and personal. We must understand this if we wish to draw from prayer what the saints call 'spiritual fruit'.

When the Christian prays on the events of sacred history, he cannot think of them as past and dead, as he can with profane history. In Tolstoy's *War and Peace* I read the description of the Battle of Austerlitz. Thanks to the talent of the author, I share the feelings of the combatants as though I were present, but I am not deceived by that. I know that this event has passed and those who lived this tragic adventure have long since turned to dust.

The feelings I experience before the events of Christ's life are different. It is not emotion such as an artist can stimulate within me by presenting events irrevocably buried in the past. I do not have to stimulate the imagination to recall them. Of course I can mentally construct a crib or look at pictures. But beyond that, I risk dwelling too much on images. They are not indispensable. They are only a means of quieting 'the mad person in the house' who always tends to distract me. By imaginative representations I give that person pasture to rest in, but the essential comes from faith. By faith I know that I am as truly present at the crib as the shepherds and wise men. Certainly I am more present at the Crucifixion than the Pharisees, who saw only with bodily eyes, and were all the while absent in heart.

This presence in faith is realised each time the event related is no longer something outside myself, but when, through grace, I feel that I live it. 'He delivered himself up for me', said St Paul. Christ is in Agony until the end of time. 'I shed this particular drop of blood for you,' Pascal has Christ say. In one way or another we must always come back to this. The event concerns me. I live it, and I am an actor in it, even if only like the little waif brought into a brilliant salon, astonished at being admitted to such a part. I recall the event Scripture relates only to take my place in it. 'Jesus looked at Peter,' says Luke after the account of the denial. He turns that same gaze on me. I am not in the presence of marvels whose remembrance makes me exclaim, 'Happy are those who witnessed this'. Rather, happy are they who do not see and who believe. The event to which they are united in faith brings them its grace of profound transformation.

Even though I remain cold as stone before the happenings in Scripture, it is not necessary to stimulate the stubborn imagination. If images have any use, it is precisely because all at once I realise that 'he is on the cross for me'. Instead of making futile efforts or ones that sidetrack me, even though they seem fruitful, I prefer to cry out my desire and weakness to God every time my mind manages to achieve some concentration. Let me say the 'today' of the Liturgy: 'God who this day revealed your glory to the peoples by the leading of a star ...' It is today, Lord, that you revealed your glory to the peoples. May I live the Lord's Epiphany as in the present moment. This plea places me on the solid soil of faith in the ever-present reality of God's action for me and for humanity.

What we say about the Gospel event we also have to say about all the words from Scripture which the Church puts on our lips to speak to God. The psalm I sing is no longer David's. I go beyond the particular story of his sin. I am talking about myself. It is with my own sin in mind that I cry to God. This is the way we should repeat these words we have said so often. The truths formulated in the prayer of the Psalms will not penetrate within us until life makes them real. There are many examples of Christians initially unmoved by the Psalms who re-discovered them when age revealed an unsuspected wretchedness in themselves. Then it seems as though these words were written 'just for me'. Since we never finish becoming ourselves, we can pick up the same words years later and find new relish in them. Their grace has not changed, but through our interior deepening, we have become more receptive to it.

After what has just been said, we realise that mere reading is not enough. Real application is required – application of the heart, not of the intellect alone. When the intellect works, it is not so much to elaborate beautiful thoughts as to apply to itself the reality proposed to it. More precisely, no matter how we attach ourselves to the object, we are present to it as we are to the Body of Christ. Try to pray this way. Immerse yourself in deep silence and in God's presence. After begging for his grace, without moving – almost as if the slightest movement could distract an attention that is still very fragile – consider a Scripture passage that you love and know well. Say the words very slowly without worrying about finishing the chapter in the time given to prayer. Think in turn that the Holy Spirit says these words to you or that he draws them out of your heart. You will soon feel the benefit of such a way of proceeding, and, more precious a blessing than any imagined, it will free you from interior problems, situate you in God and assure you into the bargain an unexpected result: the discovery of vocal prayer. God himself puts the words into your mouth and makes them penetrate the heart. According to the expression of Cassian, the monk saying the Psalms rediscovers them in himself and recites them as though they were his own. In this way the artificial opposition we raise between vocal and mental prayer vanishes. When they are defined this way, they are only two complementary aspects of a single reality: this going out of ourselves which establishes us in God.

Taken up again after a lapse of years, such a prayer is not wearisome, even if it still applies itself to the same words. It grows with the passing of time and with the wisdom which grace, in the flow of events, places in our hearts. We are amazed sometimes by the depth of simple people who, without study or special formation, judge life from the standpoint of eternity. This is because every day they have received the word of the Gospel as the light of their lives. They have come to judge people and things as God himself does, with a mingling of severity and goodness. They would be very surprised if we expressed admiration of them, for prayer has placed them so much outside self and recollected in God who has become the centre of their lives.

This long work is accomplished only in the humble of heart. A scholarly reading leaves the heart in its dryness, if it is not humble. In any case it is inoperative. It might nourish a certain religious vanity that is satisfied with the admiration of its own small world. But the force of God's word remains unknown when one wants to capture it instead of receive it. 'I bless you, Father, because you have hidden these things from the learned and wise and revealed them to the lowly and humble.' The humble Virgin of Israel knew the secrets of God, not the proud scribes who saw only questions and problems. Like guests at the Feast of Fools, they have no memory. They do not retain anything and do not learn from experience. Time and life are no help to them. No light reaches them from the words they repeat mechanically from childhood.

The perfect model: our Lady
Scripture gives us Mary as the perfect model of this way to pray. It represents her as pondering things in her heart. She heard Simeon speak of the sword of sorrow. Ten years later she hears Jesus' reference to the Father's business or the house of his Father – words she does not understand at the moment. Instead of forgetting, or hardening herself against them, she allows them to rest in her soul. Later at Cana she hears 'the hour' mentioned and still later during the public life they tell her of the allusion to those who do the will of

the Father, who are mother, brothers and sisters to Jesus. Little by little, like the seed of the parable falling into good soil, these words bud forth in her heart. At the foot of the cross they bear fruit. Mary understands the mystery being accomplished. While the apostles have run away, she has rejoined her son and is one with him, completely devoted to the Father's business. Her tears are not those of an inconsolable mother. The sword that pierces her heart is that of God's word which cuts to the quick, gives light and strength to overcome. In each detail of that sorrowful passion she does not blame fate but sees in everything the fulfilment of the prophecies. In the Church she is the first to understand that the Scriptures from Moses to the prophets speak only of what is taking place at this moment.

St Augustine, commenting on the Psalms, invites us to recite them as though Christ were saying them within us. He adds, 'Christ is now the head, now the body of the Church, now both at once.' How can we fail to give a special place to our Lady in this recital? She is the Church in its perfection, the soul in which the Holy Spirit finds no obstacle to his light. Long before we did, she read the Scriptures, she prayed the Psalms. You want to learn to pray with Scripture? Open it with Mary. Say the Psalms with her. You will quickly reap the benefits of such companionship. You will become capable of making up the Magnificat anew with her. Even when it is sung daily it will be new for you each day. Our Lady, Mother of Wisdom, will teach you to treasure in your heart the richness of God's word in order to draw from it, when the time comes, the strength to stand upright in the face of events.

The antiphon of the Blessed Virgin has us address her in these words: 'Rejoice, Virgin Mary. You alone in all the world have overcome all heresy.' How do we attribute such action to Mary? It is because heresy is something other than dangerous formulas in the minds of a few thinkers. It is spread everywhere in the temptation to retain from

Scripture only what justifies our way of seeing things. Then we are seeking self not God. As in all else, Mary gives us the example here of how to direct our thoughts. she looks at God before self, or rather it is in him that she seeks to know herself. She does not expurgate any portion of what God teaches her, but accepts all in the integrity of her faith. This is why she is given wisdom to know the secrets of history and of the universe.

If there is one thing our epoch needs it is certainly this docility to the Word. How many well-meaning apostles counterfeit this because they do not know how to listen? They brandish the Gospel to condemn what is not to their liking. The Church, guardian of the Scriptures, reacts to defend her treasure. As Mary did, let us continue to return to Scripture with the Church to receive the enlightenment we still need. This light, though, shines only for those who always have something to store in the cellars of memory. What can people learn from the book of the Scriptures who say, 'The Bible? Oh, I know it. Hasn't changed at all, has it?' Prayer, making them recall the marvels of God, has awakened no desire in them.

6

THE HEART THAT DESIRES

I want to see God is the title of a thick volume on Carmelite spirituality. Actually, there is no better formula to express the goal of the Holy Spirit in our education in prayer, by means of the Scriptures. Quotations are endless:

'My heart has said to you: I seek your face, Lord ... God of my heart, my desire is before you, my sighing is not hidden from you ... Let me see your glory ... I shall be satisfied when I see your glory ...'

And we cannot forget all the psalms of desire ... 'As the hart pants for the living waters ...'; or the happiness promised to those who desire: 'Happy are those who hunger ... The heart of those who desire God shall be joyful.'

Such outbursts are not the privilege of mystics. The Church, knowing this, constantly repeats in the Liturgy the teachings of the Psalms and never ceases to ask God to awaken true desire in us. But since it is not natural to us to centre our desires on heavenly goods, we must first consent to a metamorphosis. This transformation does not come about painlessly. It is a real purgatory. Yet if we agree to it, the heart experiences the state of simplicity promised to those who do not refuse to give themselves to God.

In each of these three points we are going to examine – metamorphosis, purification, simplicity – we shall verify what we have said a hundred times: prayer is not an effort of reflection. Though it requires the attention of the mind, it springs up from the most hidden regions of the heart and sets in motion all our powers. The stages traversed from admission of sin to the recalling of God's marvels lead to this plea: 'It is you I desire, O God ... Even in the night my

soul desires you and my spirit seeks you within me'
(Is 26:9).

The transformation of desire

To express our desire to God is not necessarily to pray. 'I
have prayed and God does not hear me.' He cannot hear
us. Our desires are not pure or conformed to his will. Or at
least through these petitions we should come to desiring
God more than the object for which we pray. Otherwise,
our prayer is like that of the pagan for whom knowledge
and possession of God do not matter so long as he can get
his hands on the power of which God has the secret. Our
God – he is indifferent to all the promised lands he displays
before our eyes, if through these he does not make himself
desired. The only Promised Land is God. Our desire must
be transformed. This is the work the Holy Spirit does while
he makes us pray through the Scriptures.

Whether we are considering the aspirations of Israel or
the petitions to our Lord in the Gospels, we see very
quickly that while we are mainly interested in the
immediate object of the petition – entry into the Promised
Land, success in battle, recovery from injuries, resurrection
of a dead friend – God is more concerned with the faith that
inspires the petition. The miracle is not an act of pure
philanthropy; rather it shows forth the tenderness of God
who wishes to be recognised through these signs. So he
gives to Israel the desire for a land running with milk and
honey, or to a blind person the desire to see, only to open
the heart and the eyes to another Promised Land and to
another Light.

This is true even if the object is a virtue, or what in our
language we call sanctity. More important for us than
acquiring moral perfection is to learn that only *he* achieves
in us, and *is* that desired perfection. St Paul begged to be
delivered from the thorn in his flesh. The meaning of this
petition is not important. God's refusal is the thing to note:

My grace is enough for you. In your weakness you will know my strength. Learn to hand yourself over to me. This is what the Most High repeats time after time to Israel: 'They shall know that there is only I.'

Hidden in our projects for perfection there is still much self-love. So we are condemned to pray longer for deliverance from our evil, until we realise that it is not the evil which is the stain that humiliates, but the absence of God in which we live untroubled. When, like our Lady, we make every good work that comes from our hands an occasion of praising God, we shall obtain the virtue desired. There will be no danger in possessing it, because it will not be a means of getting along without God.

God waits as long as is necessary. He permits our rebellions and our stubbornness, but he does not give way on this one point: the object of our desires must undergo a transformation. 'Son, give me your heart.' This request is addressed to each of us and to all humanity. As long as this heart he covets in order to fill it completely is attached to other goods, God is dissatisfied and our supplications do not move him. At last when we, like Moses, beg: 'Show me your ways – let me see your glory', God comes down. He comes into us to awaken an even greater desire and to purify us more and more.

'Do not rejoice because you have worked miracles or because the demons obey you', Christ said to the apostles on their return from a mission, 'but rejoice that your names are written in heaven'. To be with the Father, to glorify his name: this should be the object of our desires if we wish to have them fulfilled. 'I have glorified your name so that where I am, they also may be.' Christ, the image of the Father, has come only to awaken in us the desire for God. 'When you pray, you will say: "Our Father ... hallowed be thy name."'

We must examine ourselves in the light of these words to measure how far we are from this love, even in our desire for the Kingdom of God. We have everything to learn, as though we had just begun to love. We devote ourselves to our neighbour, but this sincere devotion is not pure enough. It is no small thing to come to love God for himself and others in the very love God has for them. It is not that our love for others is bad in some way, but our works too quickly tranquillise our conscience. We are not, we say, among those who call, 'Lord, Lord ...' and do nothing. But our charity, which wants to be active, no longer finds time to pray. Because it is not pure, it becomes an obstacle to the transformation of the heart. It is good at the start because it is spontaneous, but it limits itself to nature and to the individual. It must deny itself in order to pass into God and in him take on a new dimension. Then human love rediscovers its source – love of God.

At a meeting of married couples a worker made this remark: 'The Gospel gives us few concrete, practical details. St Peter was married. We would like to know how he treated his wife and mother-in-law.' If you reflect on it, the observation is just. The language of Scripture is human, but the orientation of its thought goes beyond the horizons of earthly life. That is what makes meditating it tiring or boring for those who limit their attention to the earth. Not that it rejects everyday cares and worries! A person responsible for many business matters will often say, 'I spent my whole meditation turning over in my mind money matters and building projects.' How could it be otherwise? Even though dedicated to God, we bear the common human condition along with our brothers. Without detaching us from it, prayer carries off in its wake our anguish and daily labours, but it forbids us to stop there. Your success, whatever kind it is, should not allow you to settle down. May your failure not discourage you or foster your revolt. Realise that things change constantly; learn to live, that is, to pass on. You go to God. Let your prayer nourish your desire. Do everything else without fear, but with this in mind.

The purgatory of prayer

How will this transformation take place without pain? The true difficulty of prayer lies there. Each time I consent to enter into it, I lay myself open to that attraction of God which draws me out of myself and the world of the present, to let me aspire to what eye has not seen nor ear heard, but what God has prepared for those he loves. This is a true purgatory where the Christian has a glimpse of the meaning of the 'nights' described by the mystics.

Whether in this world or in the other, this person that I am must be divested of self so that what is mortal will be absorbed by life (2 Co 5:4). In the life to come, however, I am submitted to this process, whether I like it or not. But in the prayer of the present life I run towards it of my own accord. To pray is to surrender oneself to the fire that must consume us.

The Scripture tells us in vain that this is the flame of love; it burns just as painfully and our mortal flesh does not consent all at once to being consumed in order to rejoin Christ in his glory. Being mortal, it does not want to pass away. That is what makes it resist prayer. If it were merely a question of accomplishing some ceremonies at appointed times – like mealtimes and hours for sleep – the flesh would yield willingly. It would offer no opposition to pleas addressed to God for success in our works, or even for the acquisition of the moral virtues of life in society. But to set oneself to pray for nothing, it would seem, only to adore God, to thank him for what he is, to do his will and not our own – that is crucifying in another way. That means a free and conscious admission that the Hour has not yet come and that all these hours that pass, holy as they may be, are only a preparation. From this viewpoint, the prayer which desires God (and it is not prayer without this desire) is the greatest of mortifications, a continual death to self in the desire for eternal life. Few understand it thus or let themselves be carried away by this prayer. However, this weight on our flesh is like the yoke of Christ; it sets us free. The liberation however is felt only afterwards. What we have present to us is the daily dying to which we must surrender.

If the desire for God should be awakened in spite of the resistance of the flesh, a new torment begins. I feel incapable of shaking off the weight which nails me to the present. The desire is one that cannot be satisfied. I cannot look at the light for which I was made; I cannot start out alone on the road leading to it. I am reduced to pleading: 'If you could only come down! Come back! When will you come? You will surely come; Your coming will transform me.... We shall be like him when we see him as he is.'

At this present moment of my existence, however, I experience the pain of knowing that I cannot add an inch to my stature. I learn at my own expense that for everything – the goal, the means of reaching it – I must depend on God, doing what is asked of me today without encroaching on tomorrow. As long as God does not take a hand in it, I can't even say what the necessary purification is. I have read the descriptions in the books, but this is profitable only if God gives me the experience of the reality.

The many forms of resistance within me that age reveals are overcome only by the happening that does not originate with me. My purification demands that I submit to the sting of time. That is why in spite of the acts of offering I might make as a necessary preliminary, I am always surprised. I had foreseen everything except that. I accepted death – but not that death. God teaches me through events. To be convinced of this I have only to reread the history of Israel. In Deuteronomy God explains very clearly through the mouth of Moses his conduct towards his people: 'I made you walk through the desert.'

That really is the way life looks to us. God makes us walk. Why? To make us humble, to test us, to know the depths of our hearts.... and so to found our confidence on a

God who in spite of detours and delays does not let us go hungry or allow us to become footsore in the midst of this weary marching.

This is the way things happen for most of us. We must even know the scandal of the believer who wants to be faithful to God and in the present moment finds only disadvantages in it. 'My feet were on the point of stumbling ... watching the wicked get rich ... their spite oozes like fat ... I tried to analyse the problem, hard though I found it ... until the day I pierced the mystery ... I had simply failed to understand ... my stupid attitude was brutish ... even so I stayed in your presence, you held my right hand ... my joy lies in being close to God' (Psalm 73).

This revelation occurs only in times of trouble, trial and correction. My heart and my flesh must not be consumed, so that I can truly say, 'My heart's Rock, my own, God forever' (Psalm 73).

Here we are back to the 'nothing' of St John of the Cross or the Beatitudes of the Gospels. We are not asked to accumulate meritorious works but rather to let the things in which we first placed our hope be taken away from us. Earthly possessions are good: 'God saw that it was good.' It is just because they are good that we risk being satisfied with them. Leave everything ... move on ... not in the spirit of the philosopher who wants self-mastery. You must leave yourself in order to let yourself be led where you do not want to to go. Woe to the rich person, who is swallowed up, incapable of desire. This person says, 'I've been on earth fifty years. I've never wanted for anything. I've never needed God. I don't see why I should pray to him.' Before God overwhelms us with gifts, we must first acknowledge our nothingness and recognise that God is all: living water, Promised Land, Jerusalem, father, mother, spouse, friends, sister, brother.

This acknowledgment is of such great worth that God seems like a mother playing hide-and-seek with her child in order to teach it to walk. God pursues the one who forgets him. Misfortune, sufferings and other events overwhelm us, but when we come to the point of desiring God, then God seems to abandon us so that our desire will be even greater – like the mother who hides in the next room so that the child who refuses to walk will run to join her. The whole history of Israel illustrates this way of acting. Its most delicate expression is the Song of Songs, so often commented upon by the mystics. The beloved has made his voice heard. The bride rushes forward to seize him, but he is no longer there. 'Have you seen him whom my heart loves?' 'We have seen him,' reply the watchers on the ramparts. 'He went out by that door.' The bride, wounded by desire, rushes in pursuit of the one who flees from her, only that he may later overwhelm her even more.

If we could only accept the happenings of the present life in this spirit. We too, in spite of our faults, have been awakened by his call. We who are religious have left all things for him. We already feel 'separated' – as though the world were far distant. Unable to turn back, we fear advancing towards a heaven we cannot lay hold of and of which we have no clear concept. Everything seems useless, and we still possess nothing. All the same, the heart does not doubt the God for whom it sighs, whose attraction it feels – a crucifying suspension between heaven and earth, solitude that prepares the encounter. How could we avoid thinking of Christ on the Cross who is never closer to his Father than in that moment of supreme abandonment?

What takes place then is nothing else than the very mystery of the Exodus or Passover, which is a summation of the entire Christian life. Christ living in our hearts by faith continues his passage to the Father and accomplishes in us what is lacking in his Passion. The goal of the silent prayer to which I give myself outside of Mass and liturgical acts is to make me conscious of all that is involved in the Sacraments I receive. Once more I discover that liturgical and personal prayer are not in conflict. The liturgy presupposes the personal prayer of the heart which deepens itself in prayer, but the heart that prays obtains the object of its desires only in the Sacraments of the Church. On the one hand the spiritual life must be sacramental; on the other, the sacramental life, if it is not to become superstitious, presupposes at least an awakening of the heart.

How many questions would be resolved if we could understand that this is where the real difficulty lies: allowing ourselves to pass through this purgatory of desire. Most of the problems we pose to ourselves admit of no solution. To the end of our lives we shall have insufficient time, we shall be plagued with worries, we shall be overcome by sleep. Let's do our best and pass on.

There may be some whose fidelity is not supported by the desire for God, but by the satisfaction of duty accomplished. Prayer attains its goal only if something breaks within us. The need to enter into prayer each day deepens the certitude that God knocks at our door daily, and the day will come when we shall have to open it wide to him.

The person who has not felt this divine traction in a dual feeling of fear and desire has not begun to pray in the Spirit. I may devote time to prayer, but to use it for my own ends and to find myself again in it.

I am not surrendering myself to God. Here it is not a question of time. If the heart is given, I may regret the lack of leisure to surrender more fully to this divine pressure, but I won't make a problem out of it. The first gift made, I will apply myself to the essential and go on, knowing that God, to whom I belong, is not held back by time.

The heart that becomes simple
Many things are made clearer and simpler by the austere purifying action of the desire that is oriented to heaven.

71

The meaning of 'religious chastity'

Many worry about disturbances they feel. Without sacrificing any of the ideal and still remaining at peace, it is enough to answer the question: In the midst of the turmoil I experience, is the desire for God rooted more deeply in my heart? Even in struggle and failure do I want God to transform me down to the most minute fibre of my being? If I can say Yes, my heart is chaste. Chastity is this very desire. My entire being is polarised by this adventure to which God invites me. Pass quickly over incidents along the road. Prayer does its work. It nourishes the chastity of desire.

The meaning of detachment

What we have said also helps us to understand detachment in a more positive and progressive way. It is not so much a rupture with things as a going beyond the natural movement urging us to possess them. It does not consist in having a dried-up heart but in knowing oneself to be a traveller and not stopping to stake out claims of ownership on anything. We can give ourselves only to the extent to which we are ourselves capable of possession. We put the cart before the horse in speaking of renunciation to those who aren't even conscious of what they are. We possess only to give ourselves, but we must first possess ourselves. Forgetting this first stage helps bring about a religious life based on fear when it should grow only in love. Prayer according to the Scriptures fosters this true detachment.

The meaning of apostolate

The prayer which is taught us by the Scriptures gives us no right to refuse any of the works confided to us, but it corrects the deviations which always threaten us. We always risk enclosing ourselves in these works, whether by being attached to their material side or by attributing them to ourselves. Prayer assures them an orientation at once heavenly and supernatural. All our apostolic formulas, varied as they are, have their source in the great words of Christ which sum up his work and ours: '... come from the Father and I go to the Father.' Our mission is to pass from this world to the true one. Without the transformation of our desires through prayer, how could we remain in the tension that held St Paul? 'I am caught in this dilemma: I want to be gone and to be with Christ ... but for me to stay alive in this body is a more urgent need for your sake.' Without the stimulation of prayer, how could we see apostolic power as anything but a draining of the grace of the Spirit? Prayer is the nerve centre which preserves the truth and vigour of our tasks.

Many grow tired of prayer because when the time comes they are afraid of the simplification that forces itself upon them. The saints prayed simply. Throughout their prayer they repeated a few phrases over and over: 'Lord, have pity ... Lord, my heart longs for you ...' St Alphonsus Rodriguez, coadjutor brother in the Company of Jesus, porter at the College of Majorca for forty years, kept repeating the word, 'Lord'. This one word carried him away into the infinite Being of God, inflamed him with love and plunged him into infinite fire which consumed him entirely.

All the saints from Moses to Father de Foucauld say the same. But we must have images and considerations to shore up our prayer. The wonder of the prayers of Scripture is that they cannot hold us back of themselves, as does everything our own imagination or intelligence tries to elaborate. Through the desire which lies hidden like fire in its lines, Scripture makes us go beyond the words, images and ideas. It uses these just as long as needed and leads beyond them. Why be afraid to follow Scripture in this transition? We shall reap better fruit. Nothing is more beneficial for action than this prayer 'in which there is no longer need to think. We need only desire with all our soul, we need only burn feebly and faithfully like the piercing, trembling flame before its Lord' (Paul Claudel). And if this desire is lacking, why not repeat tirelessly, 'Lord, awaken this desire I do not have', until you obtain the grace? 'Knock and it shall be opened to you.'

7

THE DOCILE HEART

Since prayer in the school of Scripture is a going out of oneself and a desire for God, it holds no danger of self-complacency or introspection. Because this prayer is a desire for heaven, you could say it also means leaving the world. How does this fit the apostolic heart which Christ says should remain in the world? In reality this kind of prayer fosters availability to God in us much more than it does the desire for heaven. It makes us ready to 'pass on' to the Father when he tells us the hour has come, but also it makes us, like the Son, God's co-operators in this universe – the handiwork of the Holy Spirit. The desire he inspires in us is not so much one for deliverance as for action with God. St Paul expresses this best: 'I am caught in this dilemma: I want to be gone and be with Christ, which would be very much the better, but for me to stay alive in this body is much more urgent for your sakes.' Not sure of what is better, I surrender myself to Christ. The last and most important effect of prayer is that it forms in us a docile heart – one capable of being taught and led by God.

Periodically the question arises: how do we reconcile prayer and action in our lives? From the view we take of the problem, we find only rather weak solutions. Here we go beyond the problems. Because this movement of conversion we have mentioned is effected through prayer, because we meditate on the work of God and come to desire him, God unites us to his action which is the accomplishment of his will. The duality no longer exists. Like Christ and with him we do the Father's will no matter what happens – whether or not we have time to 'get in our exercises' in peace. We are united to God because we are docile.

It is hard to describe this state of docility or familiarity with God in everyday actions. For this reason, we speak first about the dispositions which make it possible. Undoubtedly the stages through which Scripture leads us prepare us for it, but they are intrinsic to prayer. We are speaking now of an habitual disposition in action itself: what the spiritual writers call purity of intention or vigilance of the heart. When we have seen what this disposition is and how to foster it, we shall have a better understanding of how it brings us into close union with God and renders us docile to his action.

Superficial solutions

We often try to keep the heart centred on God by sprinkling our day with aspirations or short prayers. Such a practice is good. The saints have advised it. Yet it has dangers. When we have a predominant concern about thinking of God every time we do something, we risk neglecting both God and our actions. If you decide to pause every fifteen minutes to say an ejaculation at a time when you are absorbed in a book or caring for a sick person, I fear for the reading and the patient. Besides, this imposed aid to recollection – when not upheld by grace – quickly becomes an effort to rekindle feelings that no longer exist, or thoughts whose formulations escape us. Then it is nothing more than another form of self-seeking. Finally, this care for preserving recollection can mask unsuspiciously the fear of giving oneself fully in a definite task, as though action were only a last recourse to which we lend ourselves without full commitment. In all this the intention is good. What 'sins' – as we shall see – is the means taken.

Others, more realistic and less sentimental, seek union with God in action and sacrifice. Surely they are building on a solid foundation of truth. Prayer unites to God only if it reposes on works and on the gift of self to God. These are not the people who say, 'Lord, Lord!' But this time the question is: Are you sure that in your overflowing activity or in your austere life you are seeking God alone? The first group mentioned adds up ejaculatory prayers while you – you add up good works and acts of virtue. Neither group unites itself to God because each person risks seeking only self. The proof is simple: in their concern to act, as in their concern for recollection, they are tinged by impatience. If others do not imitate them they are bitter about it. While one dreads involvement in action more or less, the other dreads the solitude of prayer. It is only a penitential exercise submitted to as a duty. To both kinds of persons I say: despite all your desire, something is missing. Go down deep into your heart to weigh not the quantity but the quality of your actions. Return to the place where the Father sees and judges in secret, where thoughts and actions are purified, in such a way that you will no longer be seeking self either in prayer or in action. Then you will find God's peace. Your heart will not be pulled between prayer and action, rule and charity, between conflicting obligations whose disagreement serves as an excuse for not seeing what is right under our noses. We accomplish this by a constant search for rectitude of heart.

Union with God and rectitude of heart
Spiritual people of all times have spoken of vigilance of the heart or purity of intention. By this they understood what Scripture calls rectitude: the will to prevent any obstacle and any self-seeking from coming between God and self. Each one has described the way to develop this rectitude. However, there is danger they may contribute to the general confusion on the subject. Modern temperaments reading these writers without sufficient preparation find in them cause for confusion, anxiety, irritation. The minute analysis which they see themselves obliged to carry out before every action raises barriers of fear and impossibility. This is because they have read these authors prematurely

without having the necessary human stability. Such reading is not for the immature.

The error lies in the fact that we understand 'vigilance' and 'purification' in a human and psychological way. True, these writers state that an apostolic action is willed by God only if the heart is purified. As long as it is not, we must wait to achieve this. But to purify oneself does not consist in having the feeling of being pure. In that case it would be enough to say 'I'm sincere' in order to render an act good. Sincerity is as elastic as our conscience. We twist it to suit our own will. To merit attention this sincerity must be joined to rectitude, which is that will to submit oneself to an objection rule outside the fluctuation of the feelings.

Nor does purifying self mean picking our smallest actions to pieces. The more closely we observe what we do the more imperfection we uncover. And in spite of all that we have not advanced very much. This scrutiny is worth more than the naivety of the sincere heart which in its good conscience permits itself to do as it pleases. But exact as it is, this analysis throws us back on ourselves and leads to inaction and discouragement.

Let us try to penetrate the reality beneath these words. I purify my intention each time I make an effort to keep any obstacle from coming between God and myself, even if I can only offer him a miserable, egotistical heart and a weak will. I do not defend the evil I find in myself nor do I try to justify it. I stand defenceless before God in the midst of the surging of sensuality and the demands of pride. It is like a continual recourse to the Blood of Jesus Christ. 'You alone are just... You alone can cleanse me ... See, in evil was I born. Do not leave me in my corruption.' I make this movement towards him as many times as necessary, as often as I can. It is like an ejaculatory prayer: the same formula repeated again and again, but it is 'enriched' by all the misery that reality discloses within me. There is nothing artificial about it, for it arises out of life itself.

The spiritual writers of the Greek Church have often spoken about 'The Jesus Prayer.' This consists of repeating over and over throughout our prayer and work, 'Jesus, son of God, have pity on me, a sinner ...', in such a way that it becomes simultaneous with our breathing. This is an exercise that can be wrongly interpreted, too. Actually it is like a purifying and gladdening memory of the Lord Jesus, a cry of faith thrown out unceasingly to God, the soul's constant going out, a refusal to be closed in on self or on the present moment so that I may surrender to the Saviour's transforming grace. Even if I am not calm on the surface, I can always go beyond outward appearance and the obvious to surrender the deepest self, in the hope that Christ's grace will be poured little by little into my being. I no longer want to resist consciously, and above all I ask for light.

Here we are on neither the level of human virtue, simple mastery of self, nor the psychological level. Self-mastery is needed, and we must know ourselves as we are. But in the effort to do this, as in self-regard, there is something that goes beyond both, and this is purification of the heart. This process receives all its value from the sacrament for which it disposes us, in the sense that it has reference to the Blood of Jesus Christ and receives all its efficacy from the Sacrament of Penance. This is a simple example of something we have already said: there is spiritual perfection only in the domain of the sacraments.

In the life of St Alphonsus Rodriguez, the Jesuit lay brother, there is an admirable example of this exercise. I have never found a more perfect expression of it. He speaks about the moments of sadness he has endured. He writes, 'I place my bitterness between God and myself until he changes it into sweetness.'

You could not put each element into its place more exactly. On the one hand, I do not claim to change a feeling that imposes itself on me. I am sad. In one sense, what can I do about it? Many ways of struggling against the feeling only intensify it. On the other hand, I can't allow myself to stay this way or to take pleasure in it. So I stand back from this feeling; I objectify it, as though I did not take myself too seriously, and I give it to God – certain that if he speaks, he will calm the storm. Do this over and over again, twenty times, a hundred times. Repeat it especially when you are tempted to believe that it is leading nowhere. You will not be far from the rectitude or vigilance of which we speak. Your heart will turn ceaselessly toward God, and the means of this turning or 'passage' to the Lord will be the present moment – where you are – the action before you. Don't look for perfection elsewhere. Your sense of humour will grow (which never hurts us) and you will grow in love. You will discover that true union with God is a union of will within the action itself.

Examination of conscience: nourishing rectitude
Convinced of the value of all that has been said thus far, we shall soon give a frequently under-valued exercise its real importance. For many the examination of conscience is either a torture or a bore. They accuse themselves of not making it or of failing in zeal for it. How could it be otherwise? They see it only as a means of correcting faults and acquiring virtues. From that viewpoint it is a human means helpful for self-discipline, but one need not be a Christian to practise it. If you intend to make it a means in the spiritual life, you have to put it into another context. Examen is the putting into action of that daily dying which at all ages and in all circumstances of life constitutes our passage to God with Christ in faith. Three times a day at least, more if I can, I place myself before him to check on the orientation of my life. Many times a day I lift up my gaze and my heart to him.

Here we can see confirmed the dangers already pointed out: an annihilating stress on the psychological in an apparent purity of heart. How often concern for the examen has killed spontaneity in religious. They are afraid of anything natural. They watch themselves, consider themselves, and wind up being as annoying to themselves as they are to those around them. A smile becomes an act of virtue. They are looking for precision in their efforts, but it is only interior coquetry. The result is often crushing: dryness, hardness, hidden pride, and an incurable underlying sadness.

If the examen does not help the heart to open out, it is not because the examen itself is bad but because it is badly made. We have to revise our ideas about it from start to finish in order to go ahead in peace and joy. Then the examen will be an exercise of love like a bride's concern to be open and transparent to the one she loves. It establishes confidence and allows the apostle to dwell in truth and peace.

The state of docility: a very perfect obedience
Above all the examen makes possible the docility we consider to be the goal of true prayer. This growing vigilance over the heart sets us on the path to the only genuine union with God – that of obedience. This is not a separate or reserved virtue, but it is God's hold on the centre of our being. Since all is given, God can act, and this action is efficacious like his word. Convinced that we are never more active than when in this passivity, if it springs from the depths of the heart, we only try to surrender self more completely. Thus we find God at every instant. Whether or not we receive an order from a superior, whether the impulse comes from authority or external events, we no longer live for self but in all – in life as in death – we glorify God, sure of doing his will.

In this attitude there is no waiting for some exceptional happening, no illuminism, no faith in a special mission, but a very clear obedience. We accept the monotony of living it daily and are no more surprised than Mary was at stepping out of it to accomplish the wonders of God. He, who is all in all, can raise up sons of Abraham from the stones of the highway. Why shouldn't he use us? To sum up, living without future, from day to day in the present moment, we let God be and make the Kingdom a reality. From a distance this attitude appears to be *laisser-faire*, but actually it supposes the highest kind of activity and makes us God's co-workers. St John of the Cross describes this as a 'veritable ecstasy', in one of his nicely-put maxims that conclude the collection of his thoughts and notes. Asked one day how a person entered into ecstasy, John answered that it was in renouncing one's own will and doing God's. For ecstasy is nothing more for the soul than going out of oneself and being caught up in God, and that is what the one who obeys does. She goes out of herself and her own will and, liberated, she attaches herself to God. To go out of oneself – that is truly the main objective of our whole life. In overflowing action or consoling prayer, many do nothing but revolve around themselves.

Spiritual freedom

If all this is true, we are not surprised to find that this constant docility is accompanied by a state of interior freedom, true freedom founded on the gift of self, not false freedom based on the exclusion of everything unpleasant. The heart brushes aside or purifies all recrimination, all touchiness, all bitterness without being surprised at still feeling their effects. It entrusts itself entirely to God. How could it fail to be free – free as two beings are who have given themselves to each other at such depth, that of life and death – since nothing can separate us from the love of Christ. In the events that flow along through our days, the heart pauses a moment for a quick discernment. Then a new departure, and it moves ahead, without delaying. We are like the sailor of whom Claudel writes in his great

Odes. The sailor knows the world only through the map and the guide to its ports. Touching port for a moment, the sailor shakes hands with a few friends and then once more returns to the stretches of surging ocean, for home, is elsewhere.

Interior peace

In such freedom we obviously find peace – not the peace of those who ignore difficulties, the peace of children or lunatics or of a world which refuses to listen, but the peace God gives as the sure sign of his presence. For those of us who must act it is the most certain indication of his will. It assures that interior taste or profound relish which, as St Ignatius says, allows us to find no less devotion (i.e., no less gift of self to God) in action or study than in prayer. This peace becomes once more a source of docility to the Holy Spirit. When it fortifies my heart, I can act with strength. When it does not, I pray and purify myself to attain it. Waiting does no harm.

This peace does not guarantee that I will not make mistakes – that is my lot as a human being – but it permits me to undertake this action in peace without intransigence, without disdain, as a human act that is always transitory and so subject to improvement. The saints advise us: consult God in prayer before acting. They do not claim that God will send his angel to dictate our duty to us. The decision is ours. But if we have prayed, we shall be at peace and that will place God's seal on our action.

Life in Christ

Little by little, under the influence of this continually renewed purification, we come to realise the meaning of that 'life in Christ' of which St Paul speaks so often. 'The Christ who dwells in our hearts by faith.' This is not a special awareness of the presence of Christ in us. Such an awareness can be a special grace, but it can also be the effect of excited sensibility. Nor is it a kind of substitution through which decision and action are taken out of our hands. Our activity and our psychology remain human as long as we are on earth. They are situated in time. But no matter what we do, even in those faults which the just person commits seven times a day, over and above it all we can still give ourselves to Christ. 'I am certain of this,' says St Paul, 'neither life nor death, no angel, no prince, nothing that exists, nothing still to come, nor any power or height or depth nor any created thing can ever come between us and the love of God made visible in Christ Jesus our Lord.'

Nothing can block my encounter with Christ. Even after a serious fault, if faith in the Lord has not been freely denied, we can still triumph through him who has loved us. Going beyond my own horizons, I have the certitude that Christ is stronger than all other forces. Living by the Spirit in the Church he continues to build up his body in us throughout the centuries. Who will be able to separate us then? Certainly not he! Our own weakness, perhaps? But we have given that to him so that in it he may manifest his power. 'It is no longer I who live but Christ lives in me.' The better I know myself the more I see myself in him who made me and by a conversion of heart I surrender myself to him to be more completely possessed by his Spirit. 'I in him and he in me.' The discourse after the Last Supper has made such words familiar. Their realisation begins here and now.

The whole secret of the spiritual life is there. We do not surrender to Christ through lengthy prayers. These can cause many illusions. Nor is it through great undertakings, for they can conceal a great pride or a great emptiness. What we seek is to be one in all things with God's will. The feeling that this is so is a gift. It is granted only to those who renounce their own will out of love. There will never be any other way. The only purpose of elaborating on it is to shed more light, or to protect ourselves from deviations.

Each of us, accepting ourselves as we are, must always come back to this. Nature is given us only to open itself in grace.

The danger lies, not in the opening out of the seeds of life contained in our nature, but in becoming complacent about this, and nipping growth in the bud. We fulfil ourselves only in renouncing self. Some fear nature and progress. Others are afraid of renunciation as a mutilation of nature. Between these poles others seek a precarious balance. Let them enter the school of Scripture. The word of God will fill them with a wisdom which, without withdrawing them from the world, leads them beyond it, where everything finds meaning and fulfilment. They will learn not to set up a dichotomy: neither prayer with action in view, nor action to balance prayer, but a single intention in many different acts. As long as the heart maintains a continual detachment (which is the only secret of life) God who is all comes to be desired for himself alone. The heart comes and goes and is never distracted. It is in God, and God acts within it.